Employer Relations and Recruitment: An Essential Part of Postsecondary Career Services

By Myrna P. Hoover,
Janet G. Lenz, and Jeffrey W. Garis

National Career Development Association
A founding division of the American Counseling Association

NCDA opposes discrimination against any individual based on age, culture, disability, ethnicity, r
religion/spirituality, creed, gender, gender identity and expression, sexual orientation, marital/part
language preference, socioeconomic status, or any other personal characteristic not specifically re
performance. (Approved by the NCDA Board – August 2011)

No part of this book may be reproduced, stored in a retrieval system or transmitted in any form
electronic, mechanical, or photocopying, recording or otherwise, without the prior permission
Career Development Association.

Printed in the United States of America

© Copyright 2013 by the National Career Development Association
305 North Beech Circle
Broken Arrow, OK 74012
Phone: (918) 663-7060
Fax: (918) 663-7058
www.ncda.org

Library of Congress Cataloging-in-Publication Data

Hoover, Myrna P., author.
Employer relations and recruitment : an essential part of postsecondary career services /
by Myrna P. Hoover, Janet G. Lenz, and Jeffrey W. Garis.
   pages cm

ISBN 978-1-885333-39-1

1. College placement services--United States--Management. 2. College students--Vocational
guidance--United States. 3. College graduates--Employment--United States. I. Lenz, Janet G.,
1953- author. II. Garis, Jeffrey, author. III. National Career Development Association (U.S.)
issuing body.
IV. Title.
   LB2343.5.H66 2013
   331.702'35--dc23
                                         2013022851

TABLE OF CONTENTS

ACKNOWLEDGEMENTS vii
FOREWORD ix
PREFACE xi

CHAPTER 1. EMPLOYER RELATIONS HISTORY AND OVERVIEW 1
    A Brief History of Placement and Employer Relations 1
    Professional Organizations and Publications 3
    Current Mission and Philosophy 5
    Summary 6

CHAPTER 2. PROGRAM MANAGEMENT AND STRUCTURE 7
    Program Structure 7
        Centralized vs. Decentralized 8
    Program Management 9
    Staffing 10
        Events Management 11
        On-Campus Interviewing Management 12
        Job Development 12
        Additional Roles/Responsibilities 13
        Graduate Students/Peer Assistants 13
    Staff Training and Development 14
        Staff Evaluation 15
    Policies and Procedures 16
    Summary 17

CHAPTER 3. RECRUITMENT PROGRAM ACTIVITIES 19
    On-campus Recruiting 19
        Scheduling Interviews 20
        Interview Selection Procedures 21
        Bidding for On-Campus Interviews 22
        Handling Cancellations 22
        Monitoring and Communication 23
        Information Sessions and Receptions 23
        Preparing for Employers' Visits 23
        Hosting Employers on Campus 23
    Job Postings 24
        Granting Access to Job Postings 25
        Strategies for Increasing Job Postings 25

TABLE OF CONTENTS CONTINUED

    Résumé Referrals 25
    Career Fairs and Specialty Events 25
        Establishing Target Audience and Identifying
            Participants and Partners 27
        Locating a Venue and Setting a Date 27
        Allocating the Budget 27
        Marketing to Employers 27
        Marketing to Students 28
        Training Event Staff 29
        Final Steps Before the Event 29
        Event Follow-Up 31
    Credentials Service 31
    Professional Networking Databases 33
    Employer-In-Residence Programs 33
    Diversity and Leadership Programs 34
    Summary 35

CHAPTER 4. STRATEGIC MARKETING 36
    Marketing to Students 36
    Marketing to Employers 39
    Connecting to Administrators, Faculty, and Staff 41
    Determining a Cost-Effective Marketing Strategy 42
    Summary 44

CHAPTER 5. INFORMATION SYSTEMS AND TECHNOLOGY 45
    History of Technology in Employer Relations 45
    Current Premier Systems 46
    Factors to Consider in Selecting a Recruitment System 46
    Ways to Partner with Technology 51
    Funding Sources 52
    Identifying Alternative Revenue Streams to Support Technology ... 53
    Summary 53

CHAPTER 6. FUNDRAISING AND EMPLOYER RELATIONS 54
    Alternative Funding Sources 54
    Fund Generation Considerations 55
    Gaining Institutional Support for Fundraising 56
    Employer Relations Fund-Generation Programs 56

TABLE OF CONTENTS CONTINUED

    Employer Fees.. 56
    Specialized Services 56
    Advertising... 56
    Career Fairs.. 57
    Job or Internship Postings....................................... 58
    Space Utilization... 58
    Program or Event Sponsorship 58
    Employer Fundraising.. 58
    Employer Displays 58
    Employer Partner, Corporate Affinity Programs 58
    Advisory Boards 59
    Partnering with Other Institutional Development Programs ... 59
    Career Services Facility Room Sponsors 60
    Career Services Naming 60
    Unsolicited Donations 60
  Summary 60

CHAPTER 7. PROGRAM ASSESSMENT AND EVALUATION 62
  Minimal and Maximal Approaches to Evaluating Employer Relations Programs 62
    Mission Statements 63
    Annual Reports of Events and Participation 64
    Satisfaction Data 66
    Needs-Based or Nonuser Surveys 66
    Graduating Student First Destination Surveys 67
    Benchmarking.. 68
    Focus Groups.. 68
    Self-Audits 68
    External Reviews/Consultation Visits........................... 69
    Empirically-Based Outcome Assessment 70
    Advisory Boards 71
  Summary 72

CHAPTER 8. FUTURE ISSUES AND TRENDS 73
  Accountability 73
  Decentralization in Career Services 74
  Fundraising 74
  Internships.. 74

TABLE OF CONTENTS CONTINUED

    Special Populations.. 74
        Alumni.. 76
        Distance Learners.. 77
        International Students.. 77
        Veterans.. 78
    Recruiting Trends.. 78
    Virtual Recruiting/Social Media.. 80
    Summary.. 81

APPENDICES 84

Appendix A. Sample Staff Titles/Roles within Employer Relations and Recruitment Services 84

Appendix B. Sample New Employee Orientation 85

Appendix C. Sample Employee Evaluation 87

Appendix D. Sample Topics for an Employer Relations Policy and Procedures Manual 88

Appendix E. Sample Employer On-Campus Recruiting Evaluation Form 89

Appendix F. Sample Student Marketing Materials 92

Appendix G. Sample Student/Alumni Career Fair Evaluation Form 96

Appendix H. Sample Employer Handbook Topics 97

Appendix I. Sample Career Fair Employer Evaluation 98

Appendix J. Sample Employer "Hold the Date" E-mail 99

Appendix K. Sample Selected Employer Relations Publications 100

Appendix L. Sample Yearly Employer Relations Publications and Events Timeline 101

Appendix M. Sample Employer Sponsorship Opportunities 102

Appendix N. Sample Career Center Comment Card 103

Appendix O. Sample Student Veteran Career Services Information Sheet 104

ACKNOWLEDGEMENTS

We would like to thank several key people who guided and supported our work. A special thanks to NCDA who provided us with the platform and resources to share our knowledge and experiences, and to Mary Ann Powell for her project management and attentive communication. We extend our thanks to our respected colleague, Tim Luzader, who took the time from his busy schedule at Purdue to write the Foreword. We also want to thank our reviewers, Julia Makela and Robert Reardon. Julia's background in career services and higher education contributed to a thorough review of the monograph that spanned the gap of providing feedback on the smallest detail to encouraging a broader review of the issues. We would also like to express our deep appreciation for Robert Reardon whose life-long commitment, contribution, and enthusiasm for this profession transcends his work and extends to other career-services professionals by encouraging them to leave their mark through research and scholarship within this important field. Without his enthusiasm, guidance, and persistent help, this monograph would not have been possible.

Myrna P. Hoover
Janet G. Lenz
Jeff W. Garis

Myrna P. Hoover Acknowledgements
First and foremost, I would like to thank Robert Reardon for encouraging me to take on the task of writing this monograph. Without his abundant and willing support and invaluable guidance this project would not have been possible. I would also like to acknowledge my colleagues, Janet Lenz and Jeff Garis, whose collaboration and expertise made a significant contribution to this project. In particular, I would like to thank Janet Lenz for traveling on this journey with me. Her suggestions for improvement and consistent provision of the importance of this work will always be viewed as a gift. I learned a great deal from her professional and dedicated approach to this project. I want to also acknowledge prior career center directors, Jeff Garis and Bob O'Neal for giving me the opportunity to have this career. Finally, I wish to express my love and gratitude to my family—my husband Paul Hoover, sons Justin and Tyler Unger, and sister Marcia Pugh—for their understanding, encouragement, and endless love through the writing of this monograph. They are, and always will be, the wind beneath my wings. And finally, I dedicate this work to my parents who I miss every day, Ada and Mark Pugh, for giving me my wings.

Janet G. Lenz Acknowledgements
I want to express my appreciation to Myrna Hoover for inviting me on this journey with her and Jeff Garis. Myrna's knowledge of employer relations and recruitment services is second to none, and her leadership and guidance in this area has greatly contributed to my continuing education in the field. I want to acknowledge the mentorship of prior Career Center directors I have worked with from Jeff Garis, to Bob O'Neal, Richard Harwood, and Robert Shoemaker. They all helped instill in me the importance of having comprehensive career services and effectively managing employer relations. I would also like to acknowledge my

ACKNOWLEDGEMENTS CONTINUED

partner in life, work, and play, Bob Reardon, for his encouragement, his critiquing, and his unwavering love and support. Finally, I would like to acknowledge my parents, Emily and Stanley Lenz, who supported me in all things and encouraged me to follow my career path wherever it led.

Jeff W. Garis Acknowledgements

First, I would like to thank Myrna Hoover and Janet Lenz for including me in this project. It is an understatement to note that I have always respected both of these professionals and appreciate all of their contributions to Florida State University, as well as to the career development field. Bob Reardon stands as an iconic career development professional and academician who has my lifelong respect. Additionally, I would like to thank all of our staff for their support in my return in leading Penn State's Career Services. As always, I appreciate my wife Sue and our family, Jen and Gabe McKee and Greg and Annmarie Garis, for their continuing support of my professional career.

FOREWORD

First, let me be clear with the following statement: The delivery of employer relations and recruitment services is an integral part of the overall mission of the career center. While the percentage of students that seek employment upon completion of their baccalaureate degree may vary from one institution to another, all colleges and universities have a critical mass of students who desire help in making connections to prospective employers.

Consider the campus visit from an employer's experience and imagine going to a city for the very first time. You have no idea how to find the best places to eat or where to meet people, or, worse yet, how to get around. What do you do? Well, prior to arrival, you could conduct research via the Internet, but that does little to help once you're facing the obstacles and bustle in the three-dimensional world. Your best bet is to solicit help from someone who knows the city, preferably from somebody who lives there.

Therein lies the value of career centers for employers: They serve as an employer's guide to campus. And what's more, the value is more than momentary; it continues into the future as long-term relationships are nurtured. Like the fluidity of a city, a school's student organizations, faculty, and campus dynamics are in constant flux. Access channels change. Through it all, career center staff can assist employers in making critical connections and developing relationships by advising them which faculty to contact, student organizations with which to become involved, publications and websites to consider for advertisement, and events to attend and/or sponsor. Moreover, within the framework of the National Association of Colleges and Employers', *Principles for Professional Conduct*, career services practitioners can serve as highly valuable advocates for employer partners by helping them to effectively navigate the campus and tailor a recruiting strategy that matches their hiring needs.

In writing this monograph that addresses the delivery of employer relations and recruitment services, Myrna Hoover, Janet Lenz, and Jeff Garis have expertly developed an amplified roadmap helpful for both career services practitioners and stakeholders. By studying it and keeping it in a convenient location as a reference guide, readers will gain an in-depth understanding of how employer-based services are effectively delivered.

The authors introduce this monograph by describing the rich history of university placement and employer relations and the closely aligned evolution of professional organizations and publications. In doing so, they provide context by identifying the contributing factors that launched this field and helping the reader to connect the dots to previous and current labor market conditions and recruitment trends. From there, key elements relating to program management and structure are explained well with ample references to other helpful publications. Your journey continues with a thorough treatment of recruitment program initiatives ranging from varied aspects of employers' campus recruitment visits to other innovative ways to bring students and employers together.

FOREWORD CONTINUED

Given the many challenges that face career centers today, a strategic approach to marketing services and implementing technology solutions is required. An effective strategy will result in informed decision making, time efficiency, and cost savings. These two chapters in the monograph offer very useful insights and are chalked full of specific examples of marketing and technology approaches.

A respected and trusted mentor once shared with me that fund raising in support of a university career center represented a compromise with Mephistopheles. I didn't appreciate the full impact of that statement at the time. However, as I have grown as a career services professional and a university administrator, I've made it a point to not lose sight of its meaning. Given this context, I am pleased to share that you will read several practical strategies in this monograph for raising funds as part of the broader employer-relations strategy. The authors share ways in which a career center can do so in a fair and equitable way without favoring a particular employer or group of donors. The previously referenced *Principles for Professional Conduct* published by NACE offers further guidelines to help guide your fund-raising endeavors.

With increased emphasis on accountability and the expectation to deliver value, many of us in today's career services profession are assessing the value we bring to our campuses. In doing so, we find that we must address this issue in measurable ways that positively impact our institutions. The authors dedicate a chapter of this monograph to program assessment and evaluation. They discuss at length the multiple approaches that can be undertaken to evaluate employer relations programs. This section is a source of great ideas applicable to career services colleagues in all types of higher education institutions.

Finally, Myrna Hoover, Janet Lenz, and Jeff Garis gaze into a crystal ball and share with the readers what they see as the likely future of employer relations and recruitment services delivery. Given the long tenure that each of them have in our field, in combination with their intrinsic knowledge of career services–related interventions at other institutions, I'm confident that the reader will find, as I did, that their observations are insightful and will undoubtedly be spot on.

Timothy B. Luzader

Timothy B. Luzader
Director, Purdue University Center for Career Opportunities
Past President, National Association of Colleges and Employers

PREFACE

During the summer of 2011, Dr. Robert C. Reardon approached the lead author with an idea of writing a monograph to fill a gap in career services literature. His belief was that while much had been written for career development practitioners to guide their work and provide professional development, few documents existed that provided similar guidance for employer relations professionals to help them define their role and responsibilities, understand issues and trends that impact their work, and show the value of their profession within the career services field. Intrigued by the idea and with a 27-year background in employer relations, I agreed to undertake the lead role for this project. Two colleagues who also understood the importance and impact employer relations and recruitment services have on the career services field agreed to collaborate.

This monograph reviews the scope and function of employer relations and recruitment services in postsecondary career centers with an emphasis on current applications, programs, and services, and concludes with considerations of future trends and issues in the field. Even though the core mission of comprehensive career service offices has remained relatively unchanged, recruitment trends and changing market conditions have led career service professionals at most institutions to expand and reshape the scope of recruitment services offered to students and employers. While there are many organizations where employment assistance is provided, a primary setting for employer relations and recruitment activities is postsecondary institutions and this monograph will focus on that area. Although the monograph content is focused on postsecondary settings, we believe that many of the ideas can be applied in other organizations and agencies that work with job seekers and employers.

Collectively, we have more than 98 years of career services experience, primarily in large, complex universities. These kinds of institutions offer a wide range of employer relations and recruitment services because they have resources, history, staffing, and facilities to provide them. However, we realize that smaller schools may not have the capacity or mandate to offer the full range of services described in this monograph. In Chapter 3, we discuss policy analysis as the mechanism by which program goals and available resources are sorted out, realizing that some schools have fewer or different resources than others. We hope this monograph enables all career services practitioners to imagine the possibilities of what could happen in their setting.

The content focuses primarily on providing information for practitioners on the structure, policies, procedures, staffing, and evaluation of key elements that comprise employer relations and recruitment services and programs. We review the systems and technology, marketing requirements, fundraising initiatives, and outcome evaluations that support and enhance not just this program area, but also the entire career-services unit. Finally, this monograph discusses trends and issues facing career centers today within the framework

PREFACE CONTINUED

of employer relations and recruitment services. Clearly, in light of the economic changes and technological shifts, many questions remain about the future structure of employer relations and recruitment services. We hope this monograph is a contribution to this end.

Myrna P. Hoover

CHAPTER 1
Employer Relations History and Overview

The impact of an economic crisis on the global job market can make finding employment challenging for current college students and graduates. In 2009, U.S. employers reported hiring 22% fewer college graduates than the previous year. In 2010, employers hired even fewer, 7% less than 2009 (National Association of Colleges and Employers [NACE], 2009, p. 6–7). China produced 6.1 million college graduates in 2009, and 3 million of these were reported to be jobless or underemployed (Pierson, 2010). In the United Kingdom, unemployment rates have doubled for new college graduates (Loveys, 2011). Along with declining job opportunities, job seekers around the world are impacted by changes in technology and the nature of work organizations. Regardless of a person's geographic location, traditionally secure employment options are increasingly difficult to find.

While there are some signs that the worst may be over with respect to declining employment numbers, many young people and adults remain worried about their job prospects. Indeed, some sectors of the economy and some geographic regions continue to have high unemployment numbers. Career service professionals working with both student and adult job seekers are under constant pressure to identify employment opportunities for the persons they serve, be it in school settings, community, or government agencies.

We begin this chapter by providing a brief historical perspective on the field of employer relations and what was formerly known as "job placement." This chapter also reviews the past and current professional organizations and publications, and the current employer relations mission and philosophy that continue to shape the field.

A Brief History of Placement and Employer Relations

Employer relations and recruitment services have evolved to encompass services and programs that not only connect job seekers and employers, but also assist job seekers in developing the skills and tools necessary to be effective in their job search over the course of their lifetime. What once was literally an "employment agency," that primarily focused on matching people to jobs, has evolved to a "relationship agency." This programmatic shift emphasizes creating opportunities, events, and services that establish relationship linkages for job seekers and potential employers.

Formerly, known as "placement," the origin of employer relations and recruitment services in the United States traces back to the early 1900s when career services staff "placed" students (i.e., found students jobs) (Giordani, 2005; Herr, Rayman, & Garis, 1993). The first career services offices established in the United States were created to help returning World War I veterans find jobs. These college placement offices modeled themselves after the British universities' appointment secretaries, first created in the 1890s at Oxford University (NACE, n.d.). The first American version of this office is attributed to a University of Nebraska chancellor, who in 1892 created a committee of faculty responsible for placement services (Geisler, 2002). In the early 1900s, Harvard, Yale, John Hopkins, and Chicago were the first major universities to appoint full time professionals to administer a student placement office (Geisler, 2002). Prior to the establishment of these offices, faculty provided placement for graduates using the informal "old boy" network, (i.e., using social and business connections to find jobs for students) (Powell & Kirts, 1980).

While placement offices in the early 1900s focused on placing students, the U.S. depression and stock market crash of late 1920s and early

1930s changed the official role of these offices to one that was more "vocational" in nature (Giordani, 2005). Identifying employment opportunities, creating job-hunting groups, and providing more vocational information became the norm. Following World War II, veterans received financial support that enabled them to pursue further education. This large influx of veterans greatly influenced and changed the role of placement offices and their staff. Placement offices became similar to employment agencies. This shift in mission challenged them to find ways to effectively assess job seekers' skills, interests, and abilities in order to match them with jobs. The increase in U.S. college graduates, from 186,500 in 1940 to 432,058 in 1950, led universities to embrace the mission of helping graduates identify appropriate employment opportunities (Giordani, 2005). The increase in college graduates and the postwar economic growth led to an expansion of campus recruitment activities. This movement firmly solidified the need for career placement professionals to manage employers' demands for candidates and relieve faculty members of this task (Giordani, 2005).

The social and political change of the 1960s gave rise to programs that reflected more of a career development model, with less emphasis on vocational guidance approaches than previously observed (Gysbers, 1984). Placement offices expanded their roles and functions to meet the tightening demands of the job market and the changes in employment law that came with the Civil Rights Act of 1964 and Title VII (Geisler, 2002). Gone was the one-service approach to recruiting, as on-campus interviewing became one of many services. Placement offices expanded their functions to include such things as career fairs, career counseling, and career education. Students of the 1960s not only wanted to incorporate their skills into careers, they wanted careers that matched their values (Chervenik, Nord, & Aldridge, 1982). Prior to this time, placement and counseling offices typically operated as separate units. Counseling centers embraced the mission of career planning, while job placement services were often found in both student affairs and academic units. By the late 1960s, organizational change in student affairs merged these offices to embrace a developmental role focused on career planning and employment as a process (Knoll & Rentz, 1996). As a reaction to the social and economic climate of the era, placement offices shifted their emphasis from placement to career planning.

The reorganization of placement offices in the early 1960s led to the comprehensive career services offices of the 1970s and 1980s. Students began focusing on the connection between their education and future employment. Students' desire for meaningful employment shaped the next change in career services. Career offices began providing services related to skills assessments, values clarification, and decision-making skills, and became experts in teaching employment strategies (Lucas, 1986). With students' increased desire to find a "career" and not just a job, and the emerging global and mobile economy guaranteeing multiple occupations for job seekers, the mission of placement offices changed from that of "placing" students to "teaching" employability skills. Placement professionals during this time leveraged knowledge, (i.e., how to find a job, versus placing clients in jobs), and this shifting role became the foundation for the services provided through employer relations offices of today. A transformation had occurred; placement professionals no longer placed students, they taught employment skills (Geisler, 2002).

The early 1990s brought another change in career services that included an emphasis on "networking" (Dey & Real, 2010). While assessing the values and interests of students remained a career center priority, placement professionals extended their role from that of just teaching employability skills to teaching "networking" or "relationship building." Early networking strategies focused on face-to-face opportunities via career fairs, employer information sessions, and similar events (Lucas, 1986). Increased Internet capabilities and the shrinking employment marketplace propelled placement professionals to expand their use of technology to manage and provide information that would assist students in establishing and developing relationships with employers and alumni in order to obtain career information and ultimately employment. Career services offices adopted technology-based systems to support the transfer of information and contacts among students and employers (Giordani, 2005). Economic conditions, student and employer demands, and social and political changes moved the employer relations and recruitment function of career services from placing students to finding new ways to help them network. Changes in the role of placement professionals and the function of career services created the need to develop organizations and publications to support their mission (NACE, n.d.).

Professional Organizations and Publications

The first U.S.-based professional organization supporting career placement was the National Association of Appointment Secretaries organized in 1924 by May Cheney. Cheney, the first woman in the U.S. to begin a college appointment service, was elected the first president of the association, remaining in office through 1925. Eleven of the 12 founding members were women, and teacher placement was the primary mission (NACE, n.d.). The organization renamed itself the National Association of Placement and Personnel Officers in 1928, and it became the American College Personnel Association (ACPA) in 1930. It is not surprising that one of the major professional organizations for postsecondary student services has its roots in career placement.

During the late 1920s and early 1930s, regional career services professional organizations were formed in the U.S. The Eastern College Personnel Office (ECPO), the first of these organizations created, was also the first to admit employers as members and provide conferences and meetings for employers and placement officers to exchange ideas and information. "The stated objective of this new association was to promote professional improvement for its members through an interchange of information on common placement problems" (NACE, n.d.).

Regional placement and recruitment organizations continued to expand in the U.S. during the 1940s to meet the needs for increased employer recruitment activities. In 1948, one of the first unofficial national conferences for employers and practitioners occurred when General Electric invited personnel officers from large companies and placement officers from universities throughout the country to discuss issues facing both groups. From this historic meeting, the first governing guidelines for career placement services were formed. These are now known as the *Principles for Professional Practice* (Giordani, 2005). Another outcome of this conference was the creation of additional regional associations, such as the newly created Rocky Mountain College Placement Association. Ten educators had formed this association a year earlier to support the recruiting needs of employers and to form a platform for sharing information between colleges and employers. In 1948, the Southern College Placement Association and the Middle Atlantic Placement Association emerged, followed by the Midwest College Placement association in 1949 and the Western College Placement Association in 1951 (Vokac, 1999). Across the globe, higher education institutions realized the importance of ensuring the successful transition of college graduates to the workplace, and the need for connecting with employers in this process. During this same time, Canadian placement professionals established the University Counseling and Placement Association (Giordani, 2005). In Australia, a group was formed called the National Association of Graduate Career Advisory Services (NAGCAS; www.nagcas.org.au/). And, in the United Kingdom, the Association of Graduate Careers Advisory Services (AGCAS; www.agcas.org.uk) was created to "support career practitioners involved in the provision of careers and employability education."

While these associations flourished in the U.S., overlapping projects and initiatives, and a lack of communication between the groups, made it apparent that increased coordination of these regional associations would benefit everyone. Regional associations initially sought to remain autonomous, but later identified the need for a national organization to unify the regional groups and provide research and information about the profession from a national perspective (NACE, n.d.).

At the same time a national association was forming, a publication emerged, the *School and College Placement* magazine, which became the national publication of the College Placement Council. The publication of this magazine in 1940, with origins at the University of Pennsylvania, became the responsibility of the Association of School and College Placement. For ten years, Gordon A. Harwick, an insurance executive, ran the association and personally financed some operations to maintain the publication's existence. Upon Harwick's retirement in 1950, the periodical seemed doomed until Fanny Mitchell, Duke University's placement director, along with E. Craig Sweeten, the University of Pennsylvania's director of placement, heeded the call to continue its publication. In 1951, during Mitchell's term as president of the Association of School and College Placement, the publication was renamed the *Journal of College Placement*. Later, this publication changed its name to the *Journal of Career Planning and Employment* and today it is recognized as the *NACE Journal* (www.naceweb.org/journal/) (Giordani, 2005).

Between 1955 and 1956, articles in the *Journal of College Placement* chronicled meetings of the regional association presidents and their desire to form an organization to safeguard the organization's interests and provide structure and policy for the profession. In June 1956, an executive committee and eight regional association boards met at Lehigh University in Bethlehem, Pennsylvania and unanimously approved the new national advisory council, retaining the name College Placement Publications Council. Subsequently, the Council moved to Pennsylvania and was charged with creating a code of standards and conducting research and disseminating information about the profession under the direction of Robert Herrick and Everett Teal. Regional organizations who were supportive of the Council's new direction met the following year (1957) at Ohio State University, which resulted in several important outcomes. A federation of the seven regional organizations, formed under the shortened name of the College Placement Council (CPC), endorsed a new publication called *College Placement Annual*. This publication is now known as *Job Choices* and provides articles on job search assistance and profiles of potential employers to students seeking information about jobs and employers (NACE, n.d.).

CPC's expansion led to the CPC Salary Survey in 1959 and a national directory of practitioners (Giordani, 2005). CPC continued to operate without change until 1972, when adoption of an organizational membership option was first offered in the U.S. In 1975, the first U.S. national meeting was held advancing the organization to a new level. Professional programs and training, legal information about hiring/employment, benchmark studies, and recognition of members' contributions to the field characterized CPC in the 1980s. Services for management training, networking opportunities and the introduction of a website further broadened CPC's scope in the 1990's (NACE, n.d.).

In 1995, in order to be more reflective of its membership, the organization changed its name to the National Association of Colleges and Employers (NACE) and the six regional organizations followed suit (NACE, n.d.). A final restructuring occurred between 2005 and 2007 that merged the six organizations into four regional associations: Eastern Association of Colleges and Employers (EACE), Southern Association of Colleges and Employers (SoACE), Midwest Association of

Colleges and Employers (MidwestACE), and Mountain and Pacific Association of Colleges and Employers (MPACE) (Vokac, 1999).

NACE continues to serve college and employer members, setting standards for the profession and guiding the profession's future. While ACPA emerged from the beginnings of the "placement" profession, it evolved to represent all student affairs professionals working towards the advancement of lifetime learning for students (Vokac, 1999). NACE became the leading U.S. association for employment information, setting the standards that guide career center employer relations professionals and employers charged with college relations and recruiting.

The history of career services associations and publications clearly reflects the expanding role of employer relations and recruitment services. Current organizations that support career services (e.g., NACE, ACPA, NCDA) have evolved to meet both the needs and the changes of the profession and its mission.

Current Mission and Philosophy

Employer relations and recruitment services exist in most career centers and provide a resource for students seeking employment in part-time, internship, cooperative education, and full-time positions, as well as assistance in preparing applications to graduate and/or professional schools. Clearly, the profession's early mission evolved from placement to the broader, more complex area of assistance with transitions out of the educational institution, whether involving employment or continued education. With this evolution in mission and the movement of the placement function and its services from separate areas of the university into a unit within student affairs, a comprehensive and developmental approach arose for delivering these services. Career services professionals are currently tasked with the extremely important process of helping students "choose and attain personally rewarding careers and helping employers develop effective college relations programs which contribute to effective candidate selections for their organizations" (NACE, 2012, p. 2). At first glance, the mission of employer relations might only suggest an emphasis on providing programming and services, but a broader view shows the essence of this work revolves around the development of positive relationships, and teaching others the process of making connections in ways that lead to employment of graduates and successful hiring for employers.

One example of a career center's mission is to provide "an effective, collaborative, interdepartmental array of career services for students and other university constituents." This mission statement supports a far broader approach for employer relations than that of just creating programs and services for linkages between students and employers. Instead, today's vision of employer relations and recruitment services transcends programs and services embracing a positive environment rich in partnerships and networking opportunities for faculty, employers, and students. It involves an emphasis on the promotion of career development as a lifelong learning process where relationships form the essence of this approach. Developing positive relationships with the persons who seek to fill various kinds of positions in diverse organizations is an essential component of career services.

Whether students' first relationship with the career center is seeking assistance in finding a part-time job or choosing a major, the integration of career services is the key in providing a recurring process where every engagement moves students forward and provides them with learning experiences for future career success (Chevernik et al., 1982). While placement or recruitment services are often viewed as services for only a small population of students, the immersion of many students into these employer relations programs provides valuable learning experiences about the world of work and the students' role in it.

Summary

This chapter has provided a brief historical perspective of the field of employer relations and recruitment services within postsecondary institutions, and examined the organizations that shaped the past and current mission of this component of career services. Throughout the years, recruitment trends and changing market conditions led career service professionals to expand and reshape the scope of recruitment services offered to students and employers. The mission of employer relations and recruitment services evolved from that of a teacher "placement" function to a more comprehensive mission of employment and graduate school preparedness and assistance.

Professional organizations of this field have also developed and changed with the changing mission of employer relations. Originally created to provide members with employment information and recruitment ideas, these organizations now set the standards that guide career center employer relations professionals and employers charged with college relations and recruiting. The organizations also provide important benchmark data and metrics for the profession. It is important to remember that even though employer relations and recruitment services has changed in scope and mission, the foundation of this work has remained focused on building effective relationships to assist students and employers in reaching their goals.

References

Chervenik, E., Nord, D., & Aldridge, M. (1982). Putting career planning and placement together. *Journal of College Placement, 42,* 48–51.

Dey, F., & Real, M. (2010, September). Emerging trends in university career services: Adaptations of Casella's career centers paradigm. *NACE Journal,* 31–35.

Geisler, B. (2002). A brief history of vocational guidance & college career services. Retrieved March 15, 2010, from *Vocational guidance and college career services.* www.newfoundations.com/History/GeislerHist.html

Giordani, P. (2005, Fall). National Association of Colleges and Employers through the years: The history and origins of the Association. *NACE Journal, 66,* 15-18.

Gysbers, N. C. (1984). Major trends in career development theory and practice. In N. Gysbers and Associates (Eds.). *Designing careers* (pp. 618–632). San Francisco, CA: Jossey-Bass Inc.

Herr, E. L., Rayman, J. R., & Garis, J. W. (1993). *Handbook for the college and university career center.* Westport, CT: Greenwood Press.

Kroll, J., & Rentz, A. L. (1996). *Student affairs practice in higher education.* Springfield, IL: Charles C. Thomas Publishers.

Loveys, K. (2011, January 27). One in five graduates out of work as unemployment rates for university leavers doubles. *DailyMail online.* Retrieved from www.dailymail.co.uk/news/article-1350780/University-leavers-unemployment-rates-double-1-5-graduates-work.html

Lucas, E. B. (1986). College career planning and placement center: Finding their identity. *Journal of Career Development, 13*(1), 9–16.

National Association of Colleges and Employers. (n.d.). NACE organizational history. Retrieved from www.naceweb.org/About/NACE_Organizational_History.aspx

National Association of Colleges and Employers. (2009, November). *Job Outlook 2010.* Bethlehem, PA: Author. p. 6-7.

National Association of Colleges and Employers.(2012). *Principles for professional practice.* Retrieved from www.naceweb.org/principles/?referal=knowledgecenter&menuID=203, p. 2.

Pierson, D. (2010, February 18). Young, educated and jobless in China. *Los Angeles Times.* Retrieved from http://articles.latimes.com/2010/feb/18/business/la-fi-china-grads19-2010feb19

Powell, C., & Kirts, E. (1980). *Career services today: A dynamic college profession.* Bethlehem, PA: The College Placement Council.

Vokac, R. B. (Ed.). (1999, August). MidwestACE: A 50-year history. Retrieved from www.mwace.org/ContentManager/uploads/mwace_50_year_history.pdf.p.4

CHAPTER 2
Program Management and Structure

This chapter focuses on key components of an employer relations and recruitment service. One of the primary issues in program management is the organizational structure and the staffing patterns associated with any particular program structure. Many factors may influence the type of staffing patterns that are included in the employer relations and recruitment area, and examples of these are discussed. A related topic is the extent to which the employer relations is part of a centralized or decentralized career-services operation.

Also, any discussion of employer relations program management would not be complete without a review of selected policies and procedures associated with this function, including topics such as guidelines for employer and student engagement, policies related to managing on campus recruiting, expos, cash handling, alumni relations, and related activities. An examination of employer relations program functions must be in the context of the larger career services "picture" and the overall organizational structure. As Herr, Heitzmann, and Rayman (2006) noted, the career center's mission will be influenced by its administrative location within the institutional structure (e.g., academic affairs, development, student affairs), the mission of that unit, as well as the mission of the institution. Furthermore, the career center leader will undoubtedly play a key role in shaping the unique configuration of services and priorities (Curran, 2012). The size and scope of a career center may to some degree dictate which functions are unique to employer relations (e.g., recruiting coordination) and which span multiple areas (e.g., marketing, communications). We begin by discussing the structure of employer relations programs within the context of career services as a whole.

Program Structure

While this monograph specifically focuses on the employer relations aspect of career services, it is useful to explore how this unit fits in the context of a comprehensive career services program (Herr et al., 2006; Schutt, 2007). Vernick, Garis, and Reardon (2000) described how a career center's primary mission usually falls along four continua, as outlined in Figure 2.1.

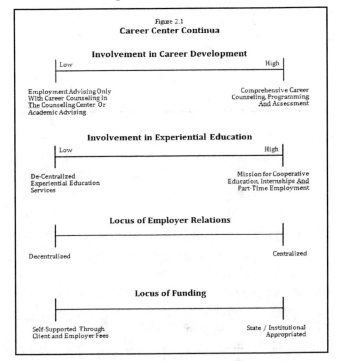

Figure 2.1. Four career center continua. From "Integrating Service, Teaching, and Research in a Comprehensive University Career Center," by S. Vernick, J. Garis, & R. Reardon, R. Copyright 2000 by *Career Planning and Adult Development Journal*. Reprinted with permission.

The first three continua include the degree to which career centers have the following components as part of their mission:

- providing career development services (e.g., career advising, counseling, assessment, information)

- providing experiential career education services (e.g., externships, internships, cooperative education)

- providing employer relations or "placement" services (e.g., career fairs, on-campus recruiting, job listings, résumé referral services)

The fourth dimension has to do with a career center's funding and the degree to which that funding is provided by the institution, external sources, or some combination. The funding reality for most modern career services offices, regardless of institutional support, is that there is an ongoing need to solicit funds from diverse sources, including key employers. Chapter 6 provides more information on how fund raising is tied to a career center's employer relations mission.

Another factor that affects the organizational structure may be the extent to which an office has a hierarchical or flat structure or some combination of the two (Herr et al., 2006). While there may be an employer relations "team," there will likely be some senior positions within that unit such as a program director or associate director. These individuals may oversee one or more assistant directors, coordinators, and support staff personnel. To provide opportunities for advancement within a specialized area of the career center like employer relations, some offices have created senior associate or assistant director positions. In turn, these individuals can supervise some lower level positions and thus avoid the situation where all the staff in a programmatic area are reporting to the unit head. Prior to discussing specific program management areas, we briefly examine the issue of centralized versus decentralized career services and how this relates to the employer relations function.

Centralized vs. Decentralized

Various sources (Herr et al., 2006; National Association of Colleges and Employers [NACE], 2012; Vernick et al., 2000; Vinson, Reardon, & Bertoch, in press) have noted that with regard to employer relations schools differ in the degree to which they have centralized versus decentralized career services operations. As Herr et al. (2006) described it, "the debate over whether career services should be centralized or decentralized has raged for years and is likely to always be an issue" (p. 138). NACE's (2012) most recent benchmarking survey of four-year institutions indicated that 84% of responding centers were centralized. The survey went on to say that "there has been a small movement toward decentralization" (p. 5).

On some campuses there may be a significant number of decentralized career services offices. Examples of this program structure can be found at the University of Texas-Austin (www.utexas.edu/academics/career-services-offices), Ohio State University (http://careers.osu.edu/employers/list-of-career-services-offices/), and the University of Illinois at Urbana-Champaign (www.careerservices.illinois.edu/careeroffices). In highly decentralized career services operations, there is usually significant variation in the degree to which a particular office, usually housed within an academic unit, provides "comprehensive" career services. Often these offices offer primarily job search support and employer relations (placement) activities for their students. Other activities in decentralized operations may be networking events and "boutique" career fairs focused on selected majors. Iowa State University describes its career services as a "coordinated network of career services offices" (www.career.iastate.edu/). On other campuses, there may be only a few decentralized units, often associated with professional or pre-professional degree programs, (e.g., engineering, law, MBA) For example, the MBA examples from Duke University's School of Business (www.fuqua.duke.edu/programs/duke_mba/cross_continent/career/) and George Mason University's School of Management (http://some.gmu.edu/mba-programs/careers/) reflect this type of structure. These offices also vary in the extent to which they "interact" with a larger, more centralized office. There may be both jointly supported and separate events.

Over the years, sources (Herr et al., 2006; Herr, Rayman, & Garis, 1993; Smith & Dey, 2010) have outlined the pros and cons of centralized versus decentralized operations. Herr et al. (2006) suggested "that high quality career services of both the centralized and decentralized variety exist; however, each has certain advantages" (p. 138).

To the extent to which there are decentralized operations, one strategy may be to have a campus "career services council" where persons representing each of these offices come together periodically to compare notes and take steps to broaden communication efforts in the interest of effectively serving students and employers. Iowa State has a council that includes as part of its charge to "facilitate communication and collaboration between career services office and university constituents" (http://www.committees.iastate.edu/comm-info.php?id=57).

The NACE (2009) evaluation standards stress the importance of having career services leaders coordinate with other career services staff off campus in order to "integrate career services into the broader educational mission" (p. 12). Adhering to this standard reinforces the idea that providing comprehensive career and employer services involves more than just reserving a few rooms to host employers who are conducting interviews. As we see the "creep" of career services into a variety of campus units, it is important to remember that there are numerous activities (e.g., professional preparation, credentials, ethical standards, and principles), associated with providing these services, and staff members involved in this type of work need to be properly trained and aware of the knowledge base in the field.

Our collective perspective is that having a "one-stop shop" serving the majority of the campus' academic units provides the best overall service delivery format to effectively meet the needs of all key stakeholders. A centralized operation makes possible a staffing structure that allows for a level of specialization across functions, thus leading to a wider variety of programs and services designed to meet the needs of all groups being served by the office. A centralized approach reduces or eliminates wasteful duplication of efforts, streamlines access to services for both students and employers, and reduces confusion for both campus and external groups. Career services and employer relations staff represent the knowledge and expertise in the field and can support the efforts of academic units in providing employment services for their students. In cases where a centralized structure is not possible or desired, the best strategy would seem to be ensuring a high level of communication between campus career services and recruiting offices. As noted earlier, the establishment of a campus career-services council, or similar entity, can help facilitate the design and delivery of employer relations and recruitment services so that the key stakeholders (i.e., students and employers) are well served.

The next section focuses on program management, including staff roles and responsibilities in the employer relations area. A key assumption is that these individuals would be functioning in a primarily centralized operation; however, they could certainly hold the same or similar roles within decentralized units.

Program Management

Program management is tied closely to what functions are specifically included under the umbrella of employer relations and recruitment services, as well as the career center's overall mission. In NACE's (2009) career services evaluation workbook, the following areas were listed under employment services:

- Career services must assist students and other designated clients in exploring a full range of career and work possibilities that match their career goals.

- Career services must assist students and other designated clients in preparing job search competencies and tools to present themselves effectively as candidates for employment.

- Career services must assist students and other designated clients in obtaining information on employment opportunities and prospective employers.

- Career services must assist students and other designated clients in connecting with employers through campus interviews, job listings, referrals, direct applications, networking, publications, and information technology.

- Career services must assist students and other designated clients in making informed choices among a variety of options.

- Career services should develop and maintain relationships with employers, alumni, and other entities that provide career development and employment opportunities for students and other clients. (p. 10)

As can be seen from this list, standards related to employer relations services within career centers go well beyond simply scheduling employers to meet with candidates. Many of these services overlap with other aspects of a comprehensive career center, particularly those that involve having job seekers clarify their career goals and make "informed choices among a variety of options" (NACE, 2009, p. 10). Each career services office will be somewhat unique in regard to how it assigns these responsibilities to staff and to what extent employer relations personnel will engage in other roles within the center (e.g., career advising and counseling, teaching career planning classes, and similar duties). The next section broadly discusses staffing issues within employer relations, as well as some key functions that must be covered as part of staffing within this area.

Staffing

"Professional staff members must have the requisite qualifications and competencies to perform effectively in their defined roles with students, alumni, faculty, administrators, and employers, as well as in highly specialized functions" (NACE, 2009, p. 20). Herr et al. (2006) described the challenges associated with managing a comprehensive career center. On the one hand, there are staff members who provide career counseling and planning services, with skill sets uniquely associated with those roles, including the National Career Development Association (NCDA) competencies for professional career counselors (NCDA, 2009). Herr et al. (2006) suggested that employer relations staff must be strongly goal-oriented, have excellent organizational skills, have an entrepreneurial spirit, and be highly extroverted. The reality for most career services offices' today, especially those with very limited staff resources, is that staff members must be competent in various roles and skills, ranging from career advising and counseling to working effectively with a variety of stakeholders, ranging from employers to family members, academic staff, and alumni.

Regardless of how staff responsibilities may be divided, a common thread that runs through all aspects of career services, and in particular employer relations, is the need for customer-relations or relations-management skills. Also, in the global economy, staff must attend to what it means for students to seek employment on a worldwide stage (Reardon, Lenz, Peterson, & Sampson, 2012). Another universal skill needed is associated with implementing and using technology, both in carrying out administrative tasks within employer relations and in assisting students. NACE's (2009) career services evaluation workbook, provides additional examples of needed skill sets that offices can benchmark against and seek to address through hiring and staff development. In addition, sample position descriptions from career services job-listing sites can provide useful data in rethinking responsibilities and essential qualifications. As position descriptions within employer relations are created and revised, it is important to ensure that the critical qualifications, knowledge, and expertise specified are matched with the essential functions in this area.

In the sections below, we discuss in more detail some of the key program-staffing areas for managing employer relations programs. Readers are encouraged to review other sections of this monograph that describe selected program functions in greater detail (e.g., on campus interviewing, fairs, fund raising, evaluation). For example, a career center may have a center-wide assessment and evaluation plan, which also includes very specific evaluation activities within employer relations that are carried out by staff in that area.

It is important to note that in smaller career services offices, many of these employer relations functions may be combined under two or three people, while on larger campuses 8–12 staff maybe involved in covering these functions. Figure 2.2 shows personnel associated with the employer relations function within the context of a career center at a large public university. Career center directors, in consultation with their staff and other unit program managers, will need to determine the unique duties associated with various employer-relations staff positions. This topic will be discussed in more detail below.

Figure 2.2. Sample Career Center Organizational Chart

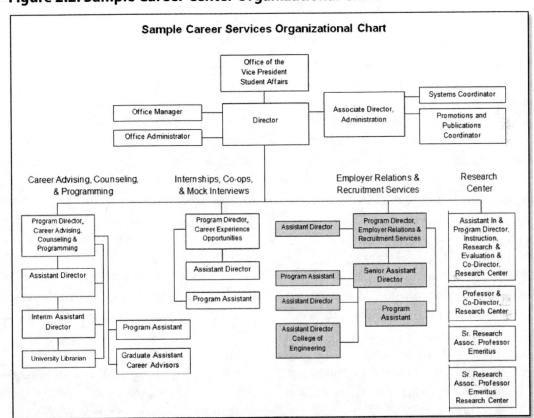

Figure 2.2. Sample career center organizational showing key functions and specific personnel titles within those functions. Adapted from the Florida State University Career Center. Reprinted by permission.

Events Management. A key component of employer relations and recruitment services involves the variety of events that bring employers to campus, including such things as career fairs, networking events, information sessions, and similar activities. While some (Collegiate Employment Research Institute [CERI], 2012) have suggested that "event planning" will decline in the years ahead as part of employer relations, there continue to be employer requests to engage with students via larger scale interactions, such as career fairs or networking events. The most recent NACE (2012) benchmarking survey noted that schools who responded typically held multiple career fairs during the course of the school year.

A number of the employer-relations sample job titles found in Appendix A include events in the title. An employer relations program must have one or more staff members who have skill sets associated with event planning. Frequent requests are also received to collaborate with an academic unit or student organization in planning and implementing events. Critical to these situations is being clear on who is handling various responsibilities (e.g., marketing, student and employer registration, setup) and how the financial aspects will be handled. It is not uncommon to see career centers recruiting and hiring individuals from the community who have had training and experience in event planning, not necessarily associated with a higher education setting (e.g., nonprofit fund raising). Event planning is a highly valuable skill that is applicable to a variety of employer relations functions.

On-Campus Interviewing Management. Within employer relations, all offices typically have one or more staff members who manage and assist with employer campus visits. Staff must manage schedules, help employers in arranging information sessions, classroom visits, and similar activities. As noted before, there is also an important customer-relations aspect for staff involved in this role, greeting employers, insuring that their day goes smoothly, and insuring that they have access to facilities and related resources for meeting one-on-one with students. This function may also involve using videoconferencing technology to help students connect with employers at a distance. Staff members overseeing this function may also coordinate data collection activities, both by having students evaluate their interviews, as well as requesting feedback from employers on the quality of students interviewed. This important role is often viewed as the "face" of the career center as more interaction with employers occurs in this role than any other.

"Job Development." Probably no area is more critical to employer relations and recruitment services than the so-called "job development" function. The success of career services offices is often evaluated by key stakeholders, including senior administrators, legislators, students, and even parents in terms of the degree to which the offices connect with employing organizations (and their job opportunities) and maintain ongoing relationships with organizations that hire the institution's graduates. From an employer's point of view, this process is increasingly referred to as talent development. While employing organizations will continue some degree of relationship with career centers, trends suggest that employers will increasingly rely on technology to drive students to their organizations and open positions (CERI, 2012). Employers will use their websites, social media, and other virtual sites to promote their organization and employment opportunities.

This topic of connecting with employers to expand job opportunities will be referenced throughout the monograph. However, it is important within the program management structure to have a key person designated to coordinate this function. In small offices, this responsibility may rest primarily with the director. In other cases, the individual who coordinates employer relations (see sample titles in Appendix A) may be charged with providing leadership in this area, as well as initial groundwork to cultivate new employers and manage ongoing relationships with existing employers. This person will work closely with the director in targeting key employers, especially when the employer outreach extends beyond job development to fundraising.

Finally, earlier in this chapter, we mentioned four continua associated with comprehensive career services. The second one related to experiential education (e.g., internships, cooperative education, part-time jobs). In some centers, this area is merged into the larger employer relations unit, since outreach to employers for these types of activities fits well with the larger employer relations and "job development" mission. If the experiential education unit exists as a separate function, it is critical that staff members in that area coordinate with employer relations staff who are targeting employers for full-time permanent positions and that all present a "united front" with regard to how employers can effectively engage all aspects of the center's programs and services to meet their needs.

Additional Roles/Responsibilities. As noted above, staff size will often drive how employer relations duties are distributed across various staff positions. Staff in this area may contribute to the center's web presence on social media sites, especially when promoting events involving employers. Employer relations personnel, along with other staff, may provide coverage for "live chat" systems maintained by the center. Staff may work with various campus departments that track on employment for targeted populations, (e.g., alumni, veterans). The position description in Figure 2.3 shows how a staff member may have targeted responsibilities within employer relations that are also combined with broader career services functions.

Figure 2.3. Senior Assistant Director, Employer Relations Sample Job Description

- Coordinate student services for employer relations recruiting program, provides outreach/orientation to students
- Write and disseminate student e-newsletter on recruitment
- Manage credentials services and alumni career services
- Oversee student registration for campus interviewing system
- Manage the student live chat feature within the on-campus interview system
- Assist in strategic planning and policy development for employer relations unit
- Provide supervision and direction to professional and clerical staff supporting recruitment, career fairs, and credentials
- Provide training and evaluation for professional and support staff
- Assist in coordinating graduate student training
- Coordinate alumni services; manage the online alumni network and serve as liaison to the alumni association; provide direct career services to alumni
- Serve as liaison to the college of human sciences; provide outreach to this population; develop and provide workshops and resources to support career planning and employment services; identify key relationships with dean, faculty, and advisors to effectively communicate with students about career opportunities
- Provide other career center services including outreach programming, career advising, and teaching the career planning course

Graduate Students/Peer Assistants. As all areas of career center services, including employer relations, have discovered, paid or unpaid graduate and undergraduate student assistants play a vital role in supporting career-center functions. Various authors have discussed the role of paraprofessionals/peer assistants in career services (Green, 2011; Herr et al., 1993; Lenz & Panke, 2001). At the lead author's institution, graduate assistant positions related to employer relations' functions are listed on the center's website: www.career.fsu.edu/about/employment/advisors/. Students can be utilized in a variety of support roles such as assisting with marketing efforts, compiling materials, preparing for events, helping with set up for career fairs, serving as "hosts" at these events, or compiling evaluation results. At many schools, both undergraduate and graduate students also serve as mock interview mentors. The use of student "ambassadors" for events such as career fairs is discussed in more detail in Chapter 3.

Each office, depending on its resources, will need to decide what number of student volunteers, interns, or other assistants is manageable given the staff time needed for training and supervision. As noted above, some positions can be paid assistantships if funding permits, other students may complete an internship and receive academic credit, while other students may simply volunteer to gain the experience and build their résumés. Students from higher education and counseling programs often fulfill these roles. While this section has provided a brief overview of staff functions, various chapters within the monograph provide greater detail on specific activities associated with these areas. Readers may use the table of contents or the index to review additional information about these topics.

Staff Training and Development

Career services and employer relations are like many areas in the private sector that are impacted by changes in the economy, global markets, and technological innovations. For that reason, staff must continually stay abreast of trends and advancements in this area (NACE, 2013). As Susan Loffredo at Northeastern University noted, "training and development must be part of a career center's culture" (NACE, 2013). Thanks to advances in technology, staff access to training on broad topics within the field is increasingly available. Within any given month, there are opportunities to view webinars and similar online presentations on the latest recruiting technology, recruiting trends, innovations in career services, and related topics. Staff memberships in professional associations such as National Association of Colleges and Employers (NACE), National Career Development Association (NCDA), National Employment Counseling Association (NECA), and similar groups provides ready access to these type of staff development opportunities.

Staff training will take many forms depending on the employee's level in the organization and the specific functions being performed. One critical step for new employees is orientation to the office, its culture, and its ways of "doing business." In the lead author's work setting, the center has long had in place a new employee orientation that includes a detailed office manual. Appendix B provides an example of what a new employee orientation process might include, what needs to happen prior to the individual's arrival, and what activities should occur once the person is on the job. An important part of this process is considering the various stakeholders that intersect with the staff member's program management areas (Sampson, 2008) and connecting the staff member with those individuals early in his or her tenure.

In the employer relations area, it is critical that new staff members build relationships with those in key academic units. There is usually a shared interest around how students in a particular academic unit will connect with employers and ultimately put their degree to work. As we note throughout this monograph, in this age of accountability, students obtaining employment following graduation is seen by key stakeholders as a measure of how well a career services and employer relations program is doing. Many career services programs have moved to a model where staff members have liaisons with specific academic and campus units. These liaisons may be reflected in staff job titles. It is critical that the career center staff member develop some measure of expertise around the liaison areas they represent. For example, if a staff member is the liaison to a particular discipline (e.g., biology, engineering, marketing, music) that staff member will know key employers and will be familiar with employment resources, websites, and other materials that can help students in that discipline obtain employment. In each academic area, it is important to know the unique challenges that students may face in job hunting (Nell, 2003). More about the idea of liaisons in career services will be discussed in Chapter 4.

As noted earlier, to stay current in the field and take advantage of professional development opportunities, employer relations and recruitment staff need to be active with their state, regional, and national associations, including such groups as NACE (www.naceweb.org), NCDA (www.ncda.org), NECA (www.employmentcounseling.org), National Association of Student Personnel Administrators (NASPA; www.naspa.org), National Association of Workforce Development Professionals (NAWDP, www.nawdp.org), and similar groups. These groups offer a variety of resources, in both print and web-based formats, that can inform good practice in the area. Some examples, developed by NACE, can be found at: www.naceweb.org/knowledge/video/2011/?refera

l=knowledgecenter&menuID=400&nodetype=4. There are webinars offered not only in real time, but also through an accessible web archive; these are very timely with regard to addressing current staff development needs.

In trying to "think outside the box" and get beyond one's own professional circles, some career center staff may choose to be involved with groups associated with other disciplines such as ones focused on human resource management, (e.g., the Academy of Management [AOM], www.aomonline.org/; or the Society for Human Resource Management [SHRM], www.shrm.org). Persons in specialized employment services will likely be involved in groups unique to the career field and disciplines they serve. Some examples of these include the MBA Career Services Council (www.mbacsc.org) and the National Association for Legal Career Professionals (NALP, www.nalp.org). Staff should be encouraged to "benchmark" their competencies against various standards in the field, such as those in the NACE (2009) career services evaluation workbook and the Council for the Advancement of Standards in Higher Education (CAS, 2012; see also www.cas.edu). Additional information related to standards and evaluation is included in Chapter 7.

Staff Evaluation. An evaluation component that provides career center employees' feedback on their performance is essential to effective functioning and continuous improvement. Most institutions operate on a one-year cycle, and in some cases have a six-month review for employees who are newly hired. Supervisors may approach this evaluation in various ways. The first consideration is how employees are performing relative to their specific position description which is on file with the institution's human resources office. There may be a standard evaluation form required by the institution. A sample of this is provided in Appendix C. Beyond the standard evaluation form, internally there may be a policy regarding employee development and the requirement that employees across all office functions develop professional goals and seek to enhance their qualifications. At the lead author's institution, that philosophy is reflected in the center's office manual as shown in Figure 2.4 below:

Figure 2.4. Promote the professional growth of Career Center staff

- Assist staff in increasing their knowledge of career development interventions through Career Advisor training, workshop presentations, and other internal Career Center training activities.
- Encourage staff members to promote a mutually supportive atmosphere for individual professional development.
- Support staff involvement in professional associations.
- Encourage staff networking within the career services profession.
- Maintain an on-going commitment to human relations training.
- Develop individual training programs and materials for new staff.
- Conduct Career Center staff meetings every two weeks during fall and spring semesters.
- Develop individual staff professional goals and objectives annually for review with supervisors.
- Conduct at least two individual staff supervision meetings each semester.
- Conduct performance appraisals with all staff annually.
- Encourage staff to participate in professional development activities that are available within the Division of Student Affairs, as well as through other University departments, (e.g., course study through academic units, Center for Continuing Education, Human Resources/Employee Assistance programs).
- Encourage staff to attend at least one professional conference or workshop annually (given available funding).
- Encourage staff to submit program proposals and present programs at professional meetings.
- Encourage staff to submit manuscripts and articles for publication in professional association journals and periodicals.

Figure 2.4. Example of staff professional growth opportunities within a comprehensive career center. Adapted from the Florida State University's *Career Center Office Manual*, 2013. Reprinted by permission.

Beyond these center-wide staff development activities, the person who oversees employer relations may work with individual staff in that area and encourage them to set personal goals that reflect employer outreach and programming. For example, a staff member tasked with job development may agree to increase the number of employer contacts made within the year by 10%. The staff member outlines a series of steps to meet this goal, which include:

- conduct a minimum of eight employer visits within a four month period
- make phone contact with all new employer registrants
- attend at least three meetings of local employers (e.g., Economic Development Council, Chamber of Commerce breakfast, local SHRM chapter meeting)

Within the context of program management, we have discussed organizational structure and staffing. Now we turn our attention to a brief discussion of policies and procedures.

Policies and Procedures

A career services office is impacted by policies and procedures set by the larger organization (Herr, et al. 2006; Sampson, 2008; Sampson, Reardon, Peterson, & Lenz, 2004; Schutt, 2007). A career center will respond with its own set of policies and procedures that cover a variety of areas. In turn, a set of policy and procedures typically develop over time that are unique to career center functions, covering counseling and advising, experiential education, and employer relations and recruitment. Policies may reflect a center's goals and mission, as well as the "reality of practical limits and constraints" (Sampson et al. 2004, p. 197) that often determine what choices will be made within the constraints of resources, staffing, physical space, and similar factors. The career center's leadership team will play a key role in determining overall policies, while unit heads will often take the role in formulating function-specific policies which are then approved by the director or other senior staff. In some cases, these may need to be approved by senior administration within the institution.

In developing and managing employer relations and recruitment units, staff will generally need to consider implementing policies and procedures that cover a wide variety of areas. These typically fall into policies that relate to students, employers, programs/services, and/or in-house administrative details (e.g., handling money, managing records). An office may even want to have a policy on creating policies (i.e., what type of activity or issue merits a policy)? Other possible questions to consider include:

- Which staff have input on the creation of a new policy?

- Who needs to know about specific policies (is it only select staff within employer relations or is it a policy that all career services staff need to be aware of)? For example, all career services staff may need to be able to explain to students the policy associated with not showing for a scheduled employer interview, while only employer relations staff may need to know policies associated with billing employers for career fair fees.

- How do institutional policies impact specific employer relations policies? For example, if an employer wants to host an event that includes alcohol, what institutional guidelines must be considered?

- How does a career services office respond to gifts from employers or other donors who have controversial reputations or are associated with negative publicity?

- What is the process for managing policies over time? Where is the "institutional memory" kept regarding why various policies were put in place and how they have evolved over time? At the lead author's center, polices associated with employer relations are assigned a number, and dates are included at the bottom showing when the policy was first created and when the policy was last revised.

- Which policies are placed on the center's website as part of "employer or recruiter education" (e.g., www.crc.ufl.edu/employers/employerPolicies.html) and which ones are kept internal to the organization (e.g., handling student protests at career fairs)?

Space in this monograph does not permit the inclusion of a complete policy and procedures manual. The list in Appendix D highlights some key areas that should be considered for inclusion in such a manual. Readers are encouraged to contact the monograph authors for specific examples from their respective institutions as well as from schools of a similar size or nature in order to get additional samples. Many schools include employer policies on their career services website and/or in an employer handbook (e.g., www.career.fsu.edu/pubs/employer-hbk/). Student policies related to specific activities such as on-campus interviewing are often included in the campus career guide and/or posted on the website. It is often helpful to pose a question on one or more e-mail lists to gather information on policies around a particular topic. In addition, readers are encouraged to draw from the information resources of professional association websites such as naceweb.org, as well as state and regional association websites (e.g., www.mwace.org/, www.soace.org/knowledge-groups).

Summary

This chapter has provided an overview of various program management topics within the context of employer relations. The employer relations function will necessarily be influenced by the institution as well as the division it is housed in, and the mission and goals of the specific career services office. The degree to which career services and employer relations are centralized or decentralized has a significant impact on overall program management and staff roles and functions. Regardless of where the employer relations function is located, certain key functions must be addressed, including events management, recruiting, job development, marketing, technology, and program activities. Developing position descriptions that include these functions are essential, and there should be clear lines of communication among staff regarding core responsibilities, managing events, hosting recruiters, and other functions performed by all staff (e.g., providing career advising, conducting outreach activities).

The career center's leadership team will play an important role in orienting and training new staff and providing opportunities for ongoing professional development. The authors share the belief that connecting to the key professional associations in the field, such as NACE and NCDA, will lead to quality services and programs that better meet the needs of both students and employers. One of the "dangers" in this age of technology is the mindset that anyone can do employer relations, no principles need to be followed, and the task is simply one of connecting candidates to jobs. This type of philosophy can lead to issues associated with fraudulent jobs, ethical violations, and dissatisfied "customers"—both students and employers. As we noted in Chapter 1, the field has evolved to include a clear set of principles and standards, and these provide the best means of assuring quality and fairness in employer relations work. In addition, when the career services office has a clear set of policies and procedures for both general operations as well as unit specific areas, it reduces the chances of having to conduct program management in a reactive mode, and all stakeholders are likely to be better served.

References

Collegiate Employment Research Institute, Michigan State University. (2012). *Recruiting trends 2012–2013* (42nd ed.). East Lansing, MI: Author.

Council for the Advancement of Standards in Higher Education. (2012). *CAS professional standards in higher education* (8th ed.). Washington, DC: Author.

Curran, S. (2012, March 21). The career center of the future: Recruiting exceptional leaders. Retrieved from http://curranoncareers.com/career-center-future-recruiting-exceptional-leaders/

Garis, J. W., Reardon, R. C., & Lenz, J. G. (2012). Current status and future development of career centers in the United States. *Asian Journal of Counseling, 19*, 5–26.

Green, M. E. (2011, February). Training paraprofessionals in the art of the résumé critique. *NACE Journal*. Retrieved from www.naceweb.org/publications/journal/2011february/training_paraprofessionals_in_the_art_of_the_résumé_critique.aspx

Herr, E. L., Heitzmann, D. E., & Rayman, J. R. (2006). *The professional counselor as administrator: Perspectives on leadership and management of counseling services across settings.* Mahwah, NJ: Lawrence Erlbaum Associates.

Herr, E. L., Rayman, J. R., & Garis, J.W. (1993). *Handbook for the college and university career center.* Westport, CT: Greenwood Press.

Lenz, J. G., & Panke, J. (2001). *Paraprofessionals in career services* (Technical Report No. 32). Tallahassee, FL: Center for the Study of Technology in Counseling and Career Development, Florida State University. Retrieved from www.career.fsu.edu/documents/technical%20reports/Technical%20Report%2032/Technical%20Report%2032.htm

National Association of Colleges and Employers. (2009). *Professional standards for college and university career services: Evaluation workbook.* Bethlehem, PA: Author.

National Association of Colleges and Employers. (2012). *NACE 2011–12 Career services benchmark survey for four-year colleges and universities.* Bethlehem, PA: Author.

National Association of Colleges and Employers. (2013, January 23). Four strategies for staying on top of staff development. *Spotlight for Career Services Professionals*. Retrieved from www.naceweb.org/s01232013/staff-development-career-services.aspx

National Career Development Association. (2009). *Career counseling competencies.* Retrieved from http://ncda.org./aws/NCDA/pt/sd/news_article/37798/_self/layout_ccmsearch/true/

Nell, A. E. (2003). The good, the bad, and the ugly: Developing placement services for liberal arts undergraduates. *Journal of Career Development, 29*, 183–194.

Reardon, R. C., Lenz, J. G., Peterson, G. W., & Sampson, J. P., Jr. (2012). *Career development and planning: A comprehensive approach* (4th ed.). Dubuque, IA: Kendall Hunt.

Sampson, J. P., Jr. (2008). *Designing and implementing career programs: A handbook for effective practice.* Broken Arrow: National Career Development Association.

Sampson, J. P., Jr., Reardon, R. C., Peterson, G. W., & Lenz, J. G. (2004). *Career counseling and services: A cognitive information processing approach.* Belmont, CA: Brooks/Cole.

Schutt, D. A., Jr. (2007). *How to plan and develop a career center* (2nd ed.). New York: Infobase Publishing.

Smith, K. K., & Dey, F. (2010, June). *To centralize or decentralize? The question facing university career services today.* Presentation at the National Association of Colleges and Employers Annual Conference & Exposition, Orlando, FL.

Vernick, S., Garis, J., & Reardon, R. (2000). Integrating service, teaching, and research in a comprehensive university career center. *Career Planning & Adult Development Journal, 16*, 7–24.

Vinson, B. M., Reardon, R. C., & Bertoch, S. C. (in press). *Career services at colleges and universities: A 30-year replication study. Journal of College Student Development.*

CHAPTER 3
Recruitment Progam Activities

Every career center is unique, not just in structure, but also in the services offered; the employer relations and recruitment unit is no exception. While there are many variations in service delivery, several core functions remain the foundation for any effective employer relations operation. Employer relations includes providing recruitment services for organizations seeking students and alumni for career opportunities such as full-time and part-time jobs, internships, and cooperative education, as well as establishing and developing relationships with key administrators, faculty, and staff at postsecondary institutions.

This chapter describes services and activities often associated with comprehensive, campus-based employer relations programs, including (a) on-campus recruiting, (b) online job-listing services, (c) résumé referrals, (d) career fairs and specialty events, (e) credentials service, (f) professional network databases, (g) employer-in-residence programs, and (h) diversity and leadership events. The purpose, goals, strategies for implementation, and evaluation methods are discussed for each of these eight programs, and a more complete vision of employer services and its importance—not only for the career center, but for the entire educational institution—becomes apparent.

On-Campus Recruiting

On-campus interviewing programs are one of the core services within a career center's employer relations and recruitment program. Key users of this service are often large (e.g., Fortune 500 employers), local or regional organizations seeking college-educated talent to fill internship and entry-level career positions. While this service provides an effective recruitment tool for employing organizations, it often serves a very small student and alumni population. The primary recruitment focus of these hiring organizations often falls within a targeted group of occupational areas, (e.g., accounting, finance, insurance, marketing/sales, staffing, technology, engineering, management). This direct correlation between interview opportunities and certain fields of study increases some students' opportunities for employment more than others. Although many employers participating in recruiting programs and job fairs indicate their willingness to see students and alumni in any major, only a limited number of job seekers are served by on-campus recruiting programs.

A constant challenge for employer relations professionals is to communicate to students, regardless of their academic preparation, that most of these employers are seeking characteristics and skills that transcend and are not directly related to a person's field of study. NACE's *Job Outlook 2011* (National Association of Colleges and Employers [NACE], 2011) survey reported that employers seek students with verbal communication skills, a strong work ethic, teamwork skills, and analytical skills. Job candidates from all majors may possess these characteristics. Likewise, employer relations staff must encourage employers to cast a wide net when recruiting students through this program so they can capitalize on the talents of students from varied disciplines.

While on-campus interviewing programs often have difficulty attracting organizations from the majority of the career fields that interest students, they still provide a critical foundation for establishing effective relationships with employers. In turn, employers who successfully meet their hiring needs through on-campus recruiting will create partnerships that will benefit the educational institution in the future. According to NACE's *Recruiting Benchmarks Survey* (NACE, 2010), an organization's recruiting experience is the most important factor in determining where it will focus its future recruiting efforts. Consequently, assisting employers in achieving a successful and positive recruitment visit needs to be a top priority for employer relations staff.

Providing a successful on-campus interviewing program, requires clearly defined and communicated procedures and policies that support employer recruitment while providing fair and equal access for students. Scheduling interview dates and information sessions, monitoring student sign-up, providing detailed communication to students and employers, and evaluating services are key activities of this service.

Scheduling Interviews

To create a successful on-campus interviewing program, career centers must provide an effective interview scheduling system and facilities conducive to recruitment activities, build effective relationships and partnerships with employer representatives, and continuously evaluate and improve the effectiveness of the program. Scheduling on-campus employer visits is handled in various ways across different types of educational settings. A school's facilities and resources will determine their ability to purchase and implement one of several career management systems currently available, (e.g., Symplicity's Career Service Manager [CSM], College Central Network [CCN], Experience, CSO Research, Inc.'s).

A lack of resources may cause some institutions to use "homegrown" scheduling systems that are typically not as sophisticated as vendor-produced systems. Schools that develop their own interview scheduling system must have adequate campus resources to update and maintain the system. Likewise, other schools schedule employer visits using less elaborate systems that could involve simple spreadsheets and request forms. At the authors' institutions, decisions were made to use a national collaborative recruiting network for administering interviewing services for students and employers. NACElink Network, an alliance with NACE, Symplicity Corporation, and DirectEmployers Association, provides a suite of web-based recruiting services used by more than 700 college career centers and more than 3 million active employer contacts. Using an on-campus interviewing system that fits the institution is fundamental to high-quality employer services.

Employers who participate in recruitment services should be asked to review and adhere to the career center's recruitment policies and procedures, as well those described in the NACE *Principles for Professional Practice* (2012). Effectively communicating recruitment expectations and the employers' acknowledgement of these practices is the first step in providing an effective recruitment program where employers can take full advantage of the universities recruiting opportunities.

Whether scheduling employment interviews via the phone, a website, in person, or a scheduling system, it is important that the employer relations staff collect employer profiles to educate students about each organization. Next, a date for the recruitment visit is scheduled and published. Because organizations' hiring projections are often in flux, most institutions only schedule employers one semester in advance. Employers who book their campus visits early secure the best possible date for their organization and provide career centers with maximum time to publicize their visit. Institutions usually accept reservations for employer visits beginning late spring/early summer, with availability for booking a visit in the fall (end of September through November) and in the spring (first of February through April). At some institutions, limited on-campus interviewing may occur during the summer term.

After approval of an employer's request for a recruitment date, career centers typically ask employers to submit a position description and the candidate qualifications they are seeking. It is imperative that the employer relations staff person reviewing this information carefully evaluate and make recommendations on the employer's selection of majors, graduation dates, GPA requirements, and any additional selection criteria in relation to the university's ability to provide an applicant recruitment pool. For example, if an employer is hiring for a position that can be filled by students from various majors, but the employer only selects one of those majors, the employer relations staff can contact the employer and suggest that the employer expand the selection criteria in order to increase the potential applicant pool. The ultimate goal is to increase the employer's long-term recruiting success at the institution.

Employer visits are publicized to students in multiple ways: via the online system, websites, classroom announcements by faculty, employer information sessions, electronic bulletin boards, video screens in facilities across campus, targeted newsletters from career center professionals, e-letters to college liaisons and advisors, and through career fairs and specialty events. Generating a large pool of applicants for each position listing is not only critical in increasing an employer's success, but it also ensures students the maximum opportunities to interview with employers visiting the campus. Once again forming relationships to "get the word" out establishes a foundation for successfully marketing employer visits. Chapter 4 will focus in greater detail on marketing services to students, including employer visits.

Interview Selection Procedures

Career centers typically use a wide range of scheduling procedures for on-campus interviews. A common approach is to allow employers to select students for interviews through what is known as preselection and open sign-up. A less common approach is bidding. These methods are managed and coordinated most effectively through a web-based system, but may still occur via mail, phone, or in person. Preselection is a process by which employers choose students they want to interview. Most institutions give employers the option to preselect their entire schedule(s), while a few institutions still limit the number of students an employer can select. At these institutions, usually only 50% of the schedule(s) can be reserved for preselected students. Employers, who use preselection to fill their schedule, receive access to students' résumés if they have expressed an interest in interviewing with the employer's organization. Most institutions only allow students to submit their résumé if they meet the employer's criteria, (e.g., GPA, major, graduation date). Other institutions take a different approach, which includes allowing all students, whether they meet the employer's exact specified requirements or not, to participate in preselection. In other words, any registered student interested in a particular employer can submit a résumé and be considered for an interview.

Allowing any student to submit a résumé, regardless of his or her qualifications, is a policy decision that seeks to provide students with more interview opportunities. This policy allows students to market their skills and background to potential employers even when the employer requests only students in a specific major or discipline. Ultimately, because employers decide whom they wish to interview based on students' résumés and/or meeting them at career fairs, and because students usually self-select, (i.e., submit résumés only if they match the credentials requested), we believe having a policy that allows students to submit a résumé for preselection regardless of their credentials creates outcomes that are more positive for both students and employers.

This preselection policy, in addition to allowing employers to capture a wider pool of applicants, provides them with the ability to include students in their applicant pool who they meet personally at career fairs. Although not all career centers tie their career fairs to the on-campus recruiting program, by linking these events, career centers can offer employers a more effective means of selecting students by screening them prior to selection, and it provides students with an additional opportunity to sell themselves to potential employers prior to the selection deadline. Career centers adopting this approach must carefully consider the dates of their career fairs as they will affect and ultimately determine the institutions' recruitment periods.

After employers review résumés of potential candidates and select students they want to interview, the employer relations staff fills the employer's schedule(s) through e-mails and phone calls. Employers are also encouraged to follow up via e-mail with the students they selected to notify them of their selection for an interview and to provide them with any additional information about the upcoming visit, (e.g., information session, required forms, documents, testing). Some institutions allow employers to select alternates for their interview schedule. This option provides employers a second tier of students who can sign up if a preselected student decides to withdraw from the interview opportunity. This option acknowledges the employers' time commitment by allowing them to fill the interview schedule with the most viable candidates.

Most career centers offer employers "open sign-up" as a stand-alone method of filling a schedule or in conjunction with preselection as a means of filling an interview schedule. However, the employer may choose to "close" the schedule regardless of whether it completely fills. A schedule closes and becomes final once all preselected students and alternates have accepted or declined interviews. Some institutions do not allow employers to close an interview schedule. Typically, institutions who limit preselection also limit closed schedules. The intention of this approach is to increase the opportunity for all students to obtain interviews. Those institutions that have moved away from this approach have done so to meet the demands of employers who choose to recruit at institutions that provide them with the ability to control their schedules in a way that ensures that their time is spent interviewing only the students they have selected.

Employers who allow institutions to fill their schedule via open sign-up will only find students scheduled who are interested in the position and meet the stated minimum requirements (e.g., major, degree, graduation date, GPA, work authorization). Students sign up on a first-come, first-served basis.

"Bidding" for On-Campus Interviews

A bidding method of scheduling campus interviews is not frequently used. While common in the 1980s and 1990s, it appears that many institutions have phased out this approach. In short, institutions who allow bidding do so in order to let students submit a bid to interview with their top-choice employer. The premise of the bidding system is to provide a more even playing field for students regardless of GPA or major. It is common for institutions that use this method to reserve half the interview slots for students to bid, thus providing interviews to students who listed the employer as their top choice. As recruitment trends changed and employers decreased the number of schools from which they recruited, institutions no longer had the luxury to require employers to use a method that did not allow them to choose the students they wanted to interview. In conversations with colleagues from other institutions, it appears that bidding has become almost obsolete.

Handling Cancellations

Once interview appointments are set the commitment to honor interviewing arrangements rests equally with both candidates and employers. Therefore, employers who cancel their visit or make changes to their interview schedules that result in cancelled appointments are often asked to follow up with these candidates via mail or e-mails from their organization. Employers can obtain résumés through the career services office to facilitate this courtesy contact. Candidates are bound to the same courtesy, (i.e., they are required to send an apology letter if they do not give adequate notice of cancellation or do not show up for an interview). Some career centers have a policy to ban students from further on-campus interviewing after a certain number of missed interviews.

Monitoring and Communication

During the scheduling process, the employer relations staff spend a tremendous amount of time monitoring schedules and communicating with both employers and students. Not only is it imperative to publicize and educate students about the opportunities to interview, it is critical to provide employers with full schedules of informed and qualified students. Employer and student newsletters serve as reminders of important dates and deadlines, and introduce both new and current opportunities. Employer relations staff also regularly confirm interview times with both students and employers via e-mail or phone prior to campus visits.

Information Sessions and Receptions

Many employers hope to increase their visibility and pool of potential candidates by providing information sessions and receptions. Employer relations staff members can accept reservations for these sessions at the same time employers book their campus recruiting visit. Institutions may opt to use various facilities on campus including the student union, other student services buildings, and/or meeting space in academic buildings to accommodate employer requests for information sessions. The employer relations staff coordinate these arrangements and assists employers with any audio-visual and catering requests. These sessions are heavily publicized to "all" students so they can use these events as opportunities to learn about employing organizations and determine whether or not the employment options relate to their future career goals. Both the employer relations staff and other career services staff members can encourage sophomores and juniors to attend these information sessions in order to identify potential jobs and future employers.

Preparing for Employers' Visits

Providing employers with a smooth transition from the time they schedule their visit to the actual day they arrive on campus requires effective communication via both e-mail and telephone. The week prior to an employer's visit, employer relations staff provide recruiters with an update of their recruitment schedule, detailed parking information (including links to any web-based campus maps), and identify any special needs the employer may have during the visit. Several days prior to an employer visit, the employer relations unit head may want to contact recruiters to ensure that all details are in place.

Hosting Employers on Campus

During the actual recruiting visit, the employer relations staff reach out to the recruiter by "getting to know" the person, the nature of the employer's recruiting mission, employment opportunities, and organizational needs. Employer relations, much like effective sales, requires identifying the organizations' recruiting needs and offering solutions in relation to the programs and services available at the institution. Building a knowledge base of information about employers and developing positive relationships with them is the basis for effective employer relations. Strong employer relationships empower staff to educate students and link them to career opportunities that in turn create win-win situations for both recruiters and students.

Both oral and written feedback about employer relation's services and the institution's programs and students' demographics are solicited from employers. During recruiting season, recruiters are asked to provide feedback about the employer relations staff, career services programs, students, facilities, and curriculum. Results of these surveys are shared with all career services stakeholders in order to address program weaknesses and reinforce program strengths (see example in Appendix E). More about evaluation as part of employer recruitment activities is discussed in Chapter 7.

Adequate preparation, marketing, communication, and follow through by the employer relations staff ensure smooth operations during employer visits and allow the career center staff to meet the recruiting team and further strengthen these relationships. Success in hiring, effective and clear policies and procedures, top-notch facilities and logistics, and strong relationships with staff and faculty create loyalty that will continue to establish the institution as a "school of choice."

Job Postings

While on-campus interviewing consumes time and labor and involves a small number of students, job postings require much less staff effort and generally provide wider job opportunities for students in all fields of study. Many career centers have partnerships with organizations where they can increase the visibility of national, regional, and local job listings to help employers solicit candidates and provide students and alumni with a means for identifying part- and full-time, co-op, and internship positions. In addition, employers who post jobs at an institution are prime candidates to target for other recruitment services. Successful job postings often develop the first contact in forming long-term relationships with employers.

Some institutions charge employers for job postings to supplement the career center's budget, while other schools may choose not to charge employers for this service. Chapter 6 provides more details on the variety of fee-based activities in employer relations that might be used to raise additional funds for career services in general and employer relations in particular. Most schools require employers to set up an account and to agree to comply with university policies, NACE professional standards, and EEOC policies prior to providing access to post jobs.

Once an employer's account is approved, postings arrive via a web-based employer-services management system that may include multischool postings or by fax, mail, or phone directly from the employer. With multischool listings, employers may choose to target a geographic region or particular type of school that fits their recruiting needs (e.g., the top ten accounting schools). Policies may vary from school to school, but most institutions adopt a procedure whereby employer relations staff must approve postings regardless of the source.

Questionable position descriptions and/or employer profiles require careful staff review to determine if a position offers a legitimate opportunity for students and alumni. Job descriptions that use personal e-mail addresses instead of a company/agency affiliation, request personal information, (e.g., Social Security Numbers, credit card or bank account numbers), offer payments or rewards in exchange for allowing the use of a student's bank account, require an upfront fee, make big promises but can't deliver, require immediate response, or are vague with details of the work to be performed are all reasons to flag the job as fraudulent. Jobs deemed fraudulent in nature are not posted, and the employer is flagged for future reference. Occasionally, removal of jobs initially approved but later identified as fraudulent requires that all job applicants be notified. Schools should attempt to educate job seekers on how to identify fraudulent jobs through direct e-mail and by posting guidelines such as the following example:

While the Career Center works diligently to monitor jobs, occasionally postings may occur that are fraudulent. Here are some tips to identify a job that is probably a scam: You must give your credit card or bank account numbers or copies of personal documents, but you get nothing in writing. You must send payment by wire service or courier. You are offered a large payment or reward in exchange for allowing the use of your bank account, often for depositing checks or transferring money. You receive an unexpectedly large check. If you view a job posting that matches these characteristics, please contact the Career Center.

Granting Access to Job Postings

Schools may have a series of steps that users must complete prior to accessing job listings. For example, students and alumni may view job opportunities by submitting a résumé, reviewing and acknowledging the center's policies and procedures, and consenting to release of their credentials to employers. Once students have access to the job listings, they can show their interest and submit their résumé to the employer. Applicants can then submit their credentials through the web-based system, the employer's website, direct e-mail, or a combination of the methods selected by the employer.

Strategies for Increasing Job Postings

Increasing the number and scope of job postings requires constant employer solicitation and partnerships with key organizations. While some employers initiate contact with career services seeking to fill only part-time jobs or internships, the employer relations staff can seek to expand the scope of employer postings in order to gain additional opportunities for students and to increase employer use of other recruitment programs. Such ongoing "job development" creates more opportunities for students and employers. Some employers, in addition to requesting a "passive" posting of jobs, may wish to directly access a pool of candidate résumés, and the employer relations staff is critical in facilitating this process.

Résumé Referrals

While employers with immediate staffing needs can opt to post their positions via a campuses' job posting system, employers can also be given access to résumés from the office's database that match the organization's employment criteria. Employers can request student and alumni résumés for a variety of employment opportunities. Some institutions charge for this service while others provide access to candidate résumés at no cost.

Students and alumni who elect to participate in a résumé referral program will most likely have their résumé sent to employers as an Adobe PDF e-mail attachment or via hard copy. Résumés are usually not sorted by major, overall GPA, graduation date, and by citizenship status unless required by law. Many employers value this referral resource when their hiring needs are urgent. It is important to remind employers who receive these résumé packages that profile or job-status information may have changed for many of the students or alumni since they last used the system. Students whose résumés are sent to an employer should be notified of the transaction so they can prepare for a phone call or e-mail from the employer. Similar to on-campus interviewing, employers are regularly encouraged to use this service as a means of increasing their recruiting success. Use of web-based résumé referrals can give employers access to a diverse pool of students from a variety of disciplines.

Employers who request student and alumni résumés should be invited to participate in other employer services, (e.g., on-campus recruiting, job postings, career fairs). Effective employer relations staff market these services aggressively by sending student résumés to employers who post job opportunities. This strategy increases student exposure to employers and encourages employers to broaden their use of the career center's recruitment services. The employer relations program's mission remains constant, to link employers to students and alumni so all are successful in the recruitment process.

Career Fairs and Specialty Events

Another cornerstone of any employer relations office is the planning and implementation of effective career fairs, sometimes called job fairs or career expositions. Institutions may offer both general and "boutique" career fairs, (i.e., fairs that focus on a particular industry, career field, position type, or graduate and professional schools) and employer relations staff usually coordinate these events. In addition, career centers may collaborate with colleges or departments to provide these types of recruitment events in order to meet the needs of a specialized academic area or to collaborate with colleges or schools who sponsor their own career events. The array of career fairs and special events offered provides the greatest single opportunity for employers and job seekers to exchange information. At some institutions, these fairs are open to all students and alumni, even though the event may target particular disciplines or career fields, while other institutions limit the participants by major, school, or college. Selected faculty, academic advisors, and administrators can be invited to attend career fairs to develop professional contacts and to obtain current employment information for advising students. The range of campus individuals invited may depend on the size of the institution, especially if the event includes one or more meals.

Schools may offer large career fairs held both in the fall and spring semesters that include employers from for-profit, nonprofit, and government agencies who are seeking to fill full-time, co-op, and internship positions with students and alumni. These events can be offered multiple times during the year. On the lead author's campus, for example, more than 125 companies and more than 1,500 job seekers attend the school's largest exposition which occurs the day after Engineering Day, a boutique career fair designed for employers seeking primarily students and alumni in engineering and related technical disciplines. Combining this specialized or boutique event with a larger "business-focused" career fair is often the norm at other institutions.

Other "boutique" career fairs focus on linking students and alumni to representatives in specialized disciplines or programs, (e.g., graduate and professional programs, education and library-related fields, health professions). Another type of job fair that has become standard at many institutions is an event focused on part-time and temporary employment. As students face rising tuition and reductions in financial aid, these fairs have become increasingly popular as a means of helping students obtain employment opportunities with local organizations. In planning these events, career centers can partner with the local Chamber of Commerce and/or workforce center to increase visibility and attract larger numbers of employers.

As noted earlier, career centers may opt to jointly sponsor events with academic units. On the lead author's campus, partnerships with key colleges and departments (e.g., business and risk management insurance, communication and information) have led to two additional career events called "Insurance Days" and the "Communication and Information Career Fair." These events, which are supported by career center facilities, technology, and staff, bring employers to college-sponsored events and represent a specialized partnership between academic and student affairs.

In geographic areas where large employers are fewer in number or schools have a small number of job candidates, institutions may decide to form consortia or other collaborations in order to offer employers the opportunity to interview with candidates from multiple schools. Institutions within a higher education system may offer a "statewide" job fair in a central location. These events often attract more regionally-based employers and represent an additional opportunity for job candidates. In Florida, for example, ten state universities sponsor a job fair in Orlando and share in both the expenses and the income from the event (www.floridacareercenters.org/statewide-job-fair/).

Regardless of the nature of a career fair, as noted in Chapter 2's discussion of staff needs, coordinating these types of events requires strong organizational and marketing skills and effective relationships with employers, administrators, academic advisors, vendors, and student and campus groups. Laying the groundwork for hosting career fairs and similar career events requires the coordinator to establish the target audience and identify participants and partners, locate a venue and set a date, allocate the budget, market and advertise to both employers and students, and train event staff. These areas will be discussed in more detail in the sections that follow.

Establishing Target Audience and Identifying Participants and Partners

As noted above, hosting a career fair or similar event requires significant planning and coordination. Prior to moving forward with such as event, it is useful to address a series of questions, including the following:

- What is the current and projected job market? Is the career fair needed?
- Are there sufficient employers/programs to justify hosting a career fair?
- Are there enough students to market to potential employers?
- Who are the event stakeholders (e.g., faculty, campus administrators, legislators)?
- Have employers and/or academic departments requested an event?
- Are there sufficient staff, time, and resources to conduct an effective event?
- What are the outcomes expected and institutional benefits from the event *and* do they outweigh the cost?
- Are there partnerships with other units/departments/colleges to be considered?

After careful analysis and determination that the event benefits the goals and mission of the institution and the target audience, the career center must establish "buy in" from the institution's administration and/or academic colleges. This could involve identifying possible event dates, times, and locations with the venue host and then with supporting hotels and vendors.

Locating a Venue and Setting a Date

The next step in effectively planning a career fair event involves securing a location that provides space for the maximum number of participants. Too small a facility creates a myriad of problems that are very difficult to remedy. On the other hand, a facility that is too large an event site may create unneeded expense, and it may send a negative message by calling attention to how few employers are participating. A critical step is ensuring that the chosen dates do not conflict with activities, holidays, or similar events that employers might attend at other institutions. Some state institutional systems and private school consortia coordinate event management through state or regional associations to avoid date conflicts and to establish an easy recruiting schedule for the employers. Once these matters are established, the employer services staff reconfirms these tentative dates, locations, and times with all partners to ensure support and participation.

Allocating the Budget

Generating a tentative budget early in the process allows event coordinators to make good planning and purchasing decisions. Many institutions require bids from multiple vendors with the idea that they promote cost savings. Employer relations staff should carefully review contracts and establish strong vendor relationships in order to acquire quality products and services at the best possible cost. Budget items can include the facility rental, utilities, equipment (e.g., booths, tables, chairs, media, carpets), event supplies, advertising, and publications (e.g., event signage, banners, and handouts, decorations, food, labor).

Marketing to Employers

After setting the event date and budget, marketing the event to participants is paramount. Effective publicity is necessary for strong attendance by both employers and students. It is essential to explain to prospective job hunters why they should attend and what benefits they will receive. Depending on the target audience, the best strategy is to market the event first to employers who currently interview on campus, post job opportunities, attend college events, partner with the alumni association, and engage in campus life. An established relationship increases the chance of employer participation. Invitations to employers without a pre-established relationship with the institution require more research and effort, but these are necessary to increase participation and establish new opportunities for students.

Collaboration with other educational institutions, chambers of commerce, professional associations, and business groups with employer contacts can increase participation. Adding "potential" employers to the employer database creates opportunities to extend invitations to new employers for other recruitment services beyond the career event. Invitations to multiple contacts at the same organization can be an effective strategy to gain participants, along with sending invitations a second time to employers who have not yet responded. The employer services staff can offer incentives to increase early sign-up, (e.g., better booth location, lower cost), as well as "penalties" (e.g., late fee, less publicity) to discourage late registration. The earlier employers register and commit to participating in the event, the easier it is to market the event to students.

Marketing to Students

Successful marketing of career events to students requires multiple methods and communication channels. Chapter 4 will focus on marketing in greater detail, but we highlight some of the key areas here to emphasize the importance of this activity (Edds, 2008). Advertisements, signs, posters, brochures, press releases, faculty announcements, and flyers can be used to promote these events (see examples in Appendix F). E-mail blasts, posts on social media sites, text messages, brief web-based videos, tweets, and campus marquees supplement the more traditional advertisements. Many institutions offer a resource packet for effectively marketing to students. Below is a sample student marketing checklist that incorporates items from the event planning checklist used by one institution's student affairs division.

Figure 3.1. Example Event Marketing Checklist

- ❏ Advertisements
- ❏ Blackboard Front Page
- ❏ Banners
- ❏ Bookstore Bags
- ❏ Bus Ads
- ❏ Campus Newspapers
- ❏ Campus Radio Station
- ❏ Campus Signage Blitz
- ❏ Campus Dining Table Toppers
- ❏ Chalking (sidewalks)
- ❏ Department Websites
- ❏ Division of Student Affairs (DSA)
- ❏ DSA Weekly E-mail
- ❏ Electronic Boards
- ❏ E-mails to Prospective Students
- ❏ Facebook, LinkedIn, Pinterest
- ❏ Family Programs Newsletter
- ❏ Flyers
- ❏ Housing Newsletters
- ❏ E-mail lists
- ❏ Local Media
- ❏ Marquee/Campus Calendar
- ❏ Public Service Announcements (PSAs)
- ❏ Stall Stories (bathroom flyers)
- ❏ Student Ambassadors
- ❏ Student Card Kiosks
- ❏ Television
- ❏ Text Messages
- ❏ Twitter
- ❏ University Newsletter
- ❏ Videos
- ❏ "Yard" Signs
- ❏ Website

Effective marketing to students requires creative, persistent, and wide-ranging methods that are closely monitored for effectiveness.

Training Event Staff

Another critical component of successful career events involves staffing. Most career fairs require the work of volunteers including both career center staff not in employer relations and members of student organizations. Volunteer training is a critical element in the successful outcome of the event. In addition, the employer relations staff working with volunteers must be prepared to make volunteers feel appreciated and important before, during, and after the event. This may involve various types of recognition for the services provided.

Successfully recruiting student volunteers begins with the employer relations staff developing strong positive relationships with student organization leaders. Student groups served by the event are typically eager to volunteer and, by creating strong relationships with the organizations' faculty advisors, a long-term commitment to the event can be achieved. Most organizations require members to volunteer a certain number of hours per semester for a sanctioned event, so being identified as one of those events ensures obtaining not just volunteers but student participation at the event. The benefits of student volunteers' efforts may include the following:

- Increased face time with employers
- Recognition of the organization on event materials
- Recognition of individual volunteers with ribbons or special nametags
- Distribution of volunteers' résumés via e-mail, CD/DVD, online résumé book
- Letters of recognition for time and effort
- Handing out goodie bags at the end of the event
- Additional activity for students' résumés

An integrated approach to working with volunteers is another way to ensure the necessary "extra" help is available. At the lead author's institution, an Ambassador-in-Residence program allows students the opportunity to be a career center volunteer for one year. Students not only volunteer for events, but they also assist in marketing programs and services, provide office support, and cover informational shifts at career center and other institutional events.

A quality program for training volunteers creates a positive career event experience for both volunteers and event participants. Several tips for a successful training program include the following:

- Offer several volunteer training times in order to increase attendance
- Establish clear expectations for volunteers, assign roles, review event details, discuss potential event problems and possible solutions, and answer questions both in writing and verbally to maximize successful volunteer behavior
- Provide refreshments and a time to mingle during training
- Know the volunteers' names and let them know that the career center staff will make them feel like they are part of the event team

Volunteers, who understand their importance in an event's success, are effectively trained, and are given recognition, will increase your chances of a successful and productive experience for all participants.

Final Steps Before the Event

Final event preparation includes setting both employer and student expectations, preparing event handouts, and arranging logistics for the day of the event. Clear event communications from the employer relations staff one to two weeks prior to the event and on the day of the event are important for both audiences. Some examples of such information include the following:

- Time and location
- Parking arrangements

- Appropriate attire
- Benefits and objectives
- Agenda and/or schedule of activities
- Tips for a Successful Event for Students & Employers (see more info at: www.career.fsu.edu/img/pdf/Employer%20Handbook/Connect_to_Campus.pdf)

Employer and student packets should be prepared at least two days in advance of the event. Student packets should include a detailed participant list, a clear venue map, and any additional event instructions. This is a great opportunity to provide students with information about the career center's other programs or services. All student attendees should receive an event evaluation that is distributed and collected prior to students leaving the event (See Appendix G). Employer packets can include the following:

- Welcome message and agenda
- List of employer participants
- Map of venue and facilities
- *Employer Handbook* (see Appendix H)
- FAQs about event and university
- Employer event evaluation (Appendix I)
- Event coordinator's business card
- Event invoice or receipt
- Name tags or instructions for obtaining name tags
- Lunch tickets
- Reminder cards or interview schedules for upcoming visits

In addition to employer and student packets, others areas needing attention include event signage, displays, and supporting materials. Signage includes booth, registration, directional, and welcome signs. Equipment to hang the signs and assist employers in displaying their information and common event necessities include:

- Easels
- Tape
- Scissors
- Tacks
- Shipping materials
- Markers
- Pens and pencils
- Nametags
- First aid kit
- Extra banners and materials
- Packaging tape
- Extension cords

Creating permanent storage bins with materials such as the ones listed above helps the employer relations staff concentrate on other details associated with creating a successful event.

The event day requires much less work if the planning activities outlined in this section have been executed well. An event walk through the day prior to the event by the coordinator to identify any overlooked issues or potential problems allows the staff and volunteers the time needed to assist in fixing the problem and/or effectively addressing any potential issues with employers. Volunteers and staff should be stationed to greet participants as they arrive, help them locate their booth, and assist them with any additional needs. Volunteers assisting in student registration should be well versed in potential questions students may have and any potential registration problems.

There are many ways to provide and track event registration, (e.g., scantrons, sign-in sheets, QR (quick response) codes, event management sign-in kiosks). Some institutions use a commercially-developed event kiosk module that allows students and alumni to swipe their student identification cards or use their campus website ID to "sign in" to the event; this action creates a nametag with the participant's name, major, and graduation date. Employers may also use a kiosk to create a personalized name badge for the event. Regardless of the registration method, it is important to provide statistics on both the number and demographics (e.g., major, class level) of participants.

At the event, the employer relations staff's main goal is to answer questions and build positive relationships with employers whenever possible. Staff can chronicle the event by taking pictures and videos of students and employers, taking notes about changes needed for future events, and noting follow-up activity needed for specific employer contacts.

Closing the event for a "sit down" luncheon and presentation hosted by the institution is ideal. While this takes away networking time with students, it provides an opportunity for key university administrators to thank employers for their participation and to solicit participation for future programs and sponsorship opportunities. Because many employers send alumni to an event like this, it is also an opportunity to recognize graduates now working at the employing organizations. The luncheon can conclude with a raffle of door prizes from the institution (e.g., hats, shirts, coolers, mugs) as a way to thank vendors for their attendance and provide participating alumni with memorabilia from their alma mater.

Event Follow-Up

Every event requires follow-up, and the sooner thank you cards to volunteers and event partners go out the more positive impact they have. Timely distribution of event numbers and summative evaluations to all stakeholders, academic partners, employers, and even students reinforces the program's benefits. Producing event reports, comparison summaries, and proposed additions and changes ensures historical data and future improvements of the event.

Credentials Service

Credentials "files" are one of the oldest services offered by career centers. In recent years however, outsourcing this service has become more common due to the staff intensive nature of the work and the limited population it serves. Career centers can opt to have students and alumni (hereafter called users) maintain their own credentials, outsource this service to a private vendor, (e.g., Interfolio, www.interfolio.com; Credential Agent, www.credentialagent.com), or the office can provide this service for a nominal fee. Despite the costs associated with the use of an external vendor credential-file services, many schools have opted for this type of service.

Typically, credential files are used when users apply to a graduate or professional school, seek a professional position at an educational institution, or seek a position in a field such as nursing, social work, or library science. Credentials files commonly provide professional and academic records, letters of recommendation, and other documents to support one's candidacy for a particular job or graduate school. Some employers and schools require credential files in their application process and, at a user's request, copies of applicant files are mailed or sent electronically to various employers or educational institutions by the employer relations staff.

Establishing a credentials file with the career services office is an easy, systematic way for users to manage their employment search or graduate school application process. This service also saves time and effort for those recommending persons for school or employment. By using the credentials service, the recommender can electronically prepare the letter, review it and change it per user's request (i.e., only one letter needs to be written for various educational institutions and/or employers). Three letters of recommendation is the norm when applying to most graduate schools or professional positions. When applying to graduate school, professors with whom the user has studied would write these letters. When applying for employment, professors, former employers or internship supervisors, and similar individuals who know the applicant well would write these letters.

Users wishing to establish a credentials file can be provided with a list of "Helpful Hints for Establishing an Effective Credentials File" which may be unique to each institution. Materials in a credentials file typically consist of the following items:

- Letters of Recommendation
- A Research Summary (optional)
- A Program of Study (optional)
- Waiver of Right to Access Faculty Evaluations (optional)

Users should be discouraged from including transcripts in the credentials file because they are not considered official by most institutions and employers when sent from the career center.

Prior to establishing a credentials file, users are required to review policies and fee information. An initial registration fee and costs for any additional mailings are billed to the user. The number of credentials sent and pages in each mailing determine the additional fees. Some institutions manage billing in-house and while others use the student financial services office. By using the student financial services office for cash transactions, both career services and users benefit; students are able to pay the fees online, and all billing inquires or receivables are managed by student financial services. Alumni also receive the same credential services and are billed through student financial services. The only additional step for alumni is the activation of an institutional identification account for billing purposes. Policies for billing users should be established in consultation with the institution's financial services office to ensure university cash-handling compliance.

Legal considerations and regulations governing credentials files need to be clearly communicated to users of this service. For example, a credentials file is open for the users inspection at all times. Current law allows them to review and copy all materials in their file. The exception to this law is for candidate appraisals and letters marked "confidential" which are dated prior to December 31, 1973.

A "Waiver of Right to Access Faculty Evaluations" can be provided to users with a credentials file, but this waiver is optional. These types of waivers are used to protect confidentiality and privacy of faculty evaluations because some will only provide confidential evaluations and believe this is necessary to increase the credibility of the evaluation. Users may choose to waive access rights to any or all evaluations written on their behalf. Should users choose to waive their rights of access, they will not be able to view the specified documents/evaluations. The completed waiver form remains in their credential file permanently. In addition, a copy of the waiver form is attached and mailed with each evaluation where the individual has waived the right of access. Selection, search, and admissions committees find waiver information useful in their appraisal process.

Most credential files (whether electronic or not) are maintained in the career services office for a minimum period, usually up to ten years from the date of establishment. After the predetermined time, inactive files are archived, but may be reactivated by a user's request. At the lead author's career center, there are only 300 active credential files and fewer than 100 new files established each year. A decision to implement an online system to increase efficiency and decrease staff work allowed the continuation of this service. While credential files are a service that is declining in some career centers, providing networking opportunities continues to be an important resource that has increased exponentially, especially with the opportunities now available for connecting via social media groups. We discuss this topic in the next section.

Professional Networking Databases

Databases of employers, alumni, and career center "friends" who have volunteered to provide career, industry, graduate school, and employment information to current students and alumni are one of the most valuable and underutilized networking and career information resources offered by most career services. Employer relations staff, because of their "boundary spanning role," are often involved in developing and managing this information resource. These types of databases are most easily managed by software systems that allow students and alumni to search for contacts based on geographical location, industry, position, or educational background. Employers, parents, and new alumni need to be solicited each year to join this important group. Employer packets distributed during career fairs and on-campus interviewing can include a direct invitation to join. Family members can be invited to join the database during parents' weekend, new student orientation, and similar events. These networking databases provide ways for a variety of individuals to support the institution without making a financial donation. Participation simply requires registering with career services, providing a background profile, and identifying how the person wants to be contacted by those seeking information.

Students and alumni should be encouraged to use the system to learn more about potential careers, activities, and experiences that will make them more marketable and to obtain job and internship ideas for future employment. They can also use it to identify additional educational requirements, (e.g., graduate and professional school, certificate programs) to provide them with the qualifications required for their chosen field. By using these databases to research prospective career fields, students and alumni will be more informed and able to ask effective questions. A guide on informational interviewing is a useful tool in this process (see an example at www.career.fsu.edu/IMAGES/PDFS/Guides/ConductingAnInformationInterview.pdf).

Users should employ good business protocol and send network contacts a thank-you note after receiving any information or assistance. While this networking opportunity may lead to potential offers, users should be discouraged from directly soliciting employment opportunities through this program. The effectiveness of this networking opportunity is hard to measure, but anecdotal data shows positive outcomes. Connecting students and alumni to professionals with experience in career fields of interest is a powerful element in a career center's employment services. These types of networking databases provide a professional venue where students, alumni, and employers can connect. However in this social media age, similar networking groups are also forming on websites like LinkedIn (Lavruski, 2009). In a competitive job market, students and job seekers should be encouraged to use all forms of networking resources, both face-to-face and electronic.

Employer-in-Residence Programs

Some institutions employ additional programs to provide individualized opportunities for employers to increase their networking interactions with students and faculty in a focused and directed way. An example is an "employer-in-residence" program that involves hosting an employer on-campus for one or two days. During these types of visits, employers may engage in a variety of activities, including:

- **Résumé Critiques** – Employers provide résumé feedback to students who visit the center for services. Some offices may opt to have a career advisor team with the employer to offer résumé advice. The student not only gets both perspectives, but the career services staff member learns more about qualities employers look for in résumés.

- **Mock Interviews** – Employers may choose to participate in mock interviews with students and provide feedback on effective interviewing techniques.

- **Classroom Presentations** – Many career services offices have identified key faculty who welcome employers to speak to their classes. Employers who want to speak in classes can be asked to present on topics relevant to the course's learning objectives, making this option appealing to both students and faculty.

- **Workshop Presentations** – Similar to classroom presentations, career center staff can collaborate with employers to present about a predetermined job search topic to classes and/or student organizations who have requested a career service's workshop.

- **Lunch Meetings with Faculty or Student Leaders** – Many employers enjoy networking with faculty and/or student leaders over a meal. While employers typically cover the cost of the meal, employer relations staff can manage all of the arrangements.

- **"Table Sit" at Key Campus Locations** – At most institutions, table-sitting arrangements can be made in the student union, targeted college locations, or other "high student traffic" areas to enable employers to interact with students in an informal way.

- **Employer Panels in Career-Related Classes** – Many institutions offer career classes (e.g., Careers in Criminology, Careers in Communications) that expose students to career fields in that major/college, or they offer more general career development classes (e.g., Introduction to Career Development www.career.fsu.edu/courses/sds3340/). Institutionalizing employer panels in these types of classes provide employers an opportunity to share career advice and information to students. Strategic scheduling that coincides with on-campus interviewing can provide this opportunity for employers.

Securing dates, making arrangements and managing these activities will maximize the employer's visit. Opportunities for employers to meet students, improve visibility and recognition, and maintain a campus presence make this program very attractive. Exposing students to employers in less formal programs allows opportunities for them to develop strong and effective networking skills and receive valuable feedback from employers.

Diversity and Leadership Programs

While employer-in-residence programs address a desire for increased campus engagement, the creation of effective diversity and leadership events help satisfy the most often requested service, (i.e., a venue that connects employers to an institution's student leaders and diverse student populations). These events can be offered in various ways, such as breakfasts, receptions, "reverse" career fairs where student organizations staff booths and employers approach the organization for information. One of the most effective methods is a program designed to partner with campus departments in charge of engaging students in leadership and multicultural experiences. Collaborating with these departments provide institutional support and broader campus exposure for employers. This partnership allows the career center to leverage relationships with other campus units who advise and interact with a diverse student population and strong leaders.

Holding a diversity or leadership event in conjunction with the primary career fair is a strategy that can benefit both students and employers, and allows marketing to occur via career fair registration and advertising. Preregistering students for the event through targeting diverse student organizations and leadership groups is also an effective marketing strategy.

A successful format for these types of events can involve having directors from all the institutions' stakeholders, (e.g., career services, the leadership office, multicultural services) take part in welcoming participants, followed by officers from each student organization giving a brief description of their group's mission and constituency. An informal networking reception immediately following this formal opening provides a way for students and employers to connect. While it is important to encourage employers to initiate introductions with students, students should receive mandatory pre-event training so they may confidently and effectively network with employers. Conducting post-evaluations with both employers and students can identify changes needed for future events.

Summary

This chapter has provided an overview of the various services and activities employer relations offices typically provide for organizations to recruit talent. As mentioned in Chapter 2, the degree to which each institution incorporates and provides these recruitment services to both employers and students varies based on the structure of the office, size of the staff and the institution, budget, and related factors. Regardless of how recruitment services are delivered to employers and students, core functions (e.g., on-campus interviewing, online job-listing services, résumé referrals, career fairs) create the foundation for an effective employer relations and recruitment program. Additional programs that provide specialty functions (e.g., credential services, alumni databases, diversity and leadership events) should also be considered as important enhancements to the package offered by career services offices. Inherent in any effective recruitment service is the ability to create effective procedures, guidelines, policies, and evaluation methods and to continue to investigate new and innovative ways to connect employers to both students, alumni, and the campus community. Effective recruitment programs develop opportunities for long-lasting relationships that ultimately benefit employers, students, alumni, career services, and the institution.

References

Edds, C. A. (2008). *How to market career development programs and services.* Broken Arrow, OK: National Career Development Association.

Lavruski, V. (2009, July 23). *10 ways universities are engaging alumni using social media.* Retrieved from http://mashable.com/2009/07/23/alumni-social-media/.

National Association of Colleges and Employers. (2010). *Recruiting benchmarks survey.* Bethlehem, PA: Author. Retrieved from http://www.naceweb.org/SearchResult.aspx?keyword=Recruiting+benchmarks+survey

National Association of Colleges and Employers. (2011, November). *Job Outlook 2012.* Bethlehem, PA: Author, p. 6–7.

National Association of Colleges and Employers. (2012). *NACE principles for professional practice.* Bethlehem, PA: Author. Retrieved from http://www.naceweb.org/principles/

CHAPTER 4
Strategic Marketing

Strategically marketing career services, programs, initiatives, and accomplishments to students, employers, administration, and faculty continues to challenge large and small career services offices. Keeping up with communication trends and the constantly changing approaches available to career services for disseminating information can overwhelm and confuse even the savviest career services professional. Developing strong relationships with intended audiences and a clear and targeted message remain central in marketing. To offer a framework for practitioners, this chapter discusses strategies to market programs and services to students and employers, and the important role administrators and faculty play in not only promoting these programs and services but also connecting these audiences to each other.

Marketing to Students

Engaging the most important stakeholder, students, has been and will continue to be a significant challenge for most career centers (Herr, Heitzmann, & Rayman, 2006). Effective and strategic marketing is essential in encouraging students to take advantage of employment programs and recruitment services. Traditional communication and marketing methods such as e-mail, letters, posters, and classroom announcements often prove ineffective in "getting the word out" to the majority of students, yet ignoring traditional channels may dilute efforts to reach other stakeholders and the few students who still use these channels (Kubu, 2012). This dilemma is complex. Building effective communication channels and creating strong networks improves an office's chance of being heard and increases student engagement. Using any type of media requires both designated personnel and well-crafted messages (Kubu, 2012). Hiring staff responsible for managing promotions and publications is becoming more common. According to a recent benchmarking survey, a little over 26% of the career centers surveyed employ staff in marketing-related positions with another 20% using part-time staff for this purpose. Figure 4.1 reflects a sample job description demonstrating this now pivotal role within career services.

Figure 4.1. Sample Career Center Marketing-Coordinator Job Description

General Description: Provides strategic leadership, creative talent, and development for all marketing and advertising strategies. Responsible for coordination and implementation of all marketing concepts to promote the Career Center services and events to all constituents including students, alumni, employers, campus departments, faculty, and administrators.

Duties and Responsibilities:
- Oversee and coordinate all staff involvement in marketing activities.
- Supervise two marketing interns and conduct weekly meetings to discuss project progress and ventures.
- Coordinate outreach efforts to students and other departments on campus. Responsible for quarterly mailings, outreach tables, and various other feedback surveys, in order to enhance the awareness and usage of all services available to students and alumni.

Figure 4.1. Continued on next page

Figure 4.1. Sample Career Center Marketing-Coordinator Job Description *continued*

- Generate and create new marketing strategies and tactics (including program advertising, electronic mailings, and campus outreach activities) to educate students and alumni regarding Career Center programs and activities.
- Participate in the Employer Relations Team. Generate and create marketing strategies to educate employers and the business community regarding all Career Center events including On Campus Interview Program, Internship Program, Career Fairs, special events, etc.
- Send electronic "E-mail Blasts" and schedule employer "Visibility Tables," and track invoices with the office budget coordinator.
- Develop master calendar/schedule for implementation of marketing/outreach plan.
- Develop effective relationships with marketing sources (e.g., campus newspaper, academic advisors in each school, student organizations, printers) and outside vendors.
- Oversee and conduct focus groups to assess student needs and the effectiveness of marketing/ outreach plans.
- Produce and update quarterly publication of Career Center events and workshops.
- Update and maintain the Career Center's website "Events Calendar" as workshops, programs, and events develop.
- Design all Career Center event marketing materials (including flyers, posters, announcements, and invitations) using graphics software packages and/or desktop publishing applications.
- Manage the supply and purchase of Career Center promotional products.

Skills, Knowledge, and Abilities:
- Excellent verbal and written communication skills, including excellent editing and proofreading skills to produce quality marketing materials.
- Knowledge of marketing principles in targeting different audiences (students, staff, employers, etc.).
- Excellent time management skills to manage multiple projects simultaneously and meet the demands of a very busy center.
- Good working knowledge and experience with graphics and/or desktop publishing software applications, which include Adobe PageMaker, Adobe Photoshop, Adobe Illustrator, Microsoft Publisher, Microsoft PowerPoint, and others. Must also be familiar with Windows, Internet Explorer, Microsoft Word, and Excel, and have a general knowledge of database management.
- Ability to appropriately represent the University and its students to the employment community through various media.
- Ability to relate to a broad variety of individuals' ethnicities/backgrounds, and familiarity with affirmative action principles and goals.
- Knowledge of methods and techniques to facilitate student outreach activities.
- Ability to lead the development and implementation of marketing strategies involving collaborative arrangements with professional colleagues.
- Ability to work independently under minimal supervision.

As discussed in Chapter 2, finding staff with the right credentials is key to maximizing both productivity and creating a team environment. The fit between the person and the position is crucial because the marketing position has the potential to support the work of every staff member in the office. While strategic marketing is the foundation for this important role, success depends on the marketing person understanding and effectively communicating the goals and vision of both the career services center and the university. Evaluating media sources, managing information flow, and crafting the appropriate message takes strategic marketing, dedicated staff, a thorough understanding of the mission of career services, and a commitment of resources to accomplish this task (Giordani, 2012).

To reach students, career centers must go where the audience is. Today's college students tend to ignore fliers or e-mail in favor of texting and social media (Giordani, 2012). NACE's recent benchmarking survey (NACE, 2012) reported that 81% of career centers responded to this trend by using a Facebook "fan" page and almost half of the colleges employed a Twitter profile, an increase since 2010 of 59% and 36%, respectively. Even with social media becoming the primary method for communicating with students, print media (e.g., newsletters, career guides, brochures, e-mail blasts, blogs, posters) are still common methods for career services to publicize employer events and recruitment programs. With so many ways to communicate with students, it is easy to question if using too many messages in too many places at one time may dilute a career center's "brand."

As with getting messages to students about job searching, being strategic may take additional planning and time investment on the front end, but it may increase the payoff. Student feedback on career events and other programs, as well as focus groups formed to gain information about marketing strategies, are effective ways to learn not only which of these vehicles are most effective to use, but also what messages are the correct ones to send.

For years, employer relations units have spent time and money sending messages that tell students "what we do" to help them land a job. According to Graham Donald (NACE, 2006), developer of the Canadian Institute for Career Center Management, the real message we should be delivering to students is "what's in it for them" if we want them to attend career center programs and services. Communication that focuses on how to be successful finding a job or gaining acceptance into a graduate or professional school, retelling success stories of how internships led to full-time job offers, and posting videos of successful alumni telling the usefulness of engaging in career center activity emphasizes what students can achieve as opposed to just what services are provided. Student testimonials provide credibility when marketing career services (Edds, 2008). Students value programs and practices that have the students' best interest at heart (Carvalho & de Oliveira Mota, 2010), and career centers can use student success stories (see Figure 4.2) as one method to not only promote career center programs and services, but to also build student confidence in the contribution of these programs and services to their success.

Figure 4.2. Featured Student Success Stories on Career Center Website

Figure 4.2. Career center website can be used to highlight student success stories and share how career center programs and services contributed to that success. Retrieved from http://career.fsu.edu/success/. Copyright 2013 by The Florida State University Career Center. Used by permission.

Marketing must engage students where they are and it must communicate how taking advantage of career center programs and services will benefit them. Without effective marketing to students, employer-based events will not only suffer, but employers may abandon activities at the institution in order to recruit at other institutions that have developed successful strategies to help them reach students.

Marketing to Employers

Marketing to employers is also critical. Employers are both vital partners in the educational process and primary customers for college/university career services. Each career services office must develop policies and practices to ensure the highest quality employer relations and services (NACE, 2009). Effective marketing strategies must be integrated into the career services office and require developing and documenting a strategic plan for employer relations and development that includes a clear vision of the purpose and the intended results. Setting realistic, yearly goals to establish priorities and evaluate accomplishments, keeping abreast of the current economy and employers' recruiting needs, and reviewing past efforts and evaluating their success are key elements in defining goals and determining an effective marketing strategy. Many activities and outreach campaigns can assist career services professionals in successfully marketing programs and services; however, the key to successful employer marketing is creating meaningful and targeted messages and relationships.

Career services can develop successful employer partnerships by targeting employers that are highly relevant to their student populations. Knowing and marketing the institution's top programs and majors will provide a large return on investment. "Employers report that they select schools to target based on a variety of criteria, including quality of programs, recruiting experience at the school, and majors offered" (NACE, 2011). Knowing the institution's student demographic is critical. National employers may hire large numbers, but if the targeted group of students is not available at the campus, recruiting messages will prove ineffective. Likewise, targeting employers whose locations are outside of the geographic areas where the majority of graduates plan to relocate after college is a waste of time and effort. Even when a campus has enough students in a particular discipline or major to attract employers to campus recruiting events, the employer may not be able to successfully hire students.

The employer relations team needs to know the types of employment opportunities that students typically seek prior to targeting employers and developing relationships. Surveying students about the types of employers and opportunities they seek will save time and money in the long run. Investing resources at the front and crafting targeted marketing materials to promote students to the desired audience is a wise investment. Student surveys through online questionnaires, career fairs, career advising, internships, and career services workshops can be used. Surveys can also be administered through social media groups, classes, and student organizations, especially those associated with academic disciplines. Knowing the student population and their employment goals are not just important when trying to meet their needs, it is also essential in gaining the greatest return on investment when marketing to employers.

Once practitioners know their students' demographics, employment goals, and preferred employers, identifying employers to target for recruiting activities can be accomplished through numerous avenues. Regional and local resources, state and national associations, chambers of commerce, trade magazines, alumni referrals, previous employer exchanges, Society for Human Resource Management (SHRM) chapters, Toastmasters, Rotary Clubs, e-mail lists, blogs, LinkedIn, development offices, and prospects from conferences and other networking events are just a few ways to create a list of targeted employers. Also, in ways similar to marketing strategies used by financial institutions, employer relations staff can capitalize on pre-existing customers by soliciting employers to expand the products they use. If an employer already participates in one of the center's recruitment services, that initial contact with the office provides an opportunity to explain the benefits by using the full array of services. The employer relations staff need to maximize their opportunities by periodically evaluating their marketing strategies by asking questions, such as:

- Are there employers in your target group who are only posting job notices or attending job fairs but not engaging in other recruiting events?

- Are current employers interviewing for all types of opportunities, (e.g., internships, full-time and part-time positions) or have they limited their postings to just one type?

- Are some employers only networking with faculty and staff? How can these employers be persuaded to be active in center events and programs to give them broader exposure to students and alumni?

- Have previous employers stopped using recruiting services? If so, why? Have they been called to find the answer to the question and, more importantly, to discuss solutions for why they no longer recruit on the campus?

- Are there new perspective employers in the surrounding area and in the students' preferred geographic areas of employment?

- Is the employer relations staff marketing to small and mid-sized employers who meet your students' preferred employment opportunities?

- Is the office researching employers who recruit at similar schools within the region and contacting them about the local school's programs, students' characteristics, and recruitment events?

- In follow-up surveys, when students report where they obtained jobs or internships, are these employers being invited to participate in campus recruiting activities?

- Are alumni databases routinely reviewed for potential new employers?

- Is the office searching social media (e.g., LinkedIn, Facebook) for potential new employers?

An essential and consistent marketing strategy for employer relations staff involves using current relationships to develop stronger recruiting partnerships and increasing the services employers use.

Regardless of the type of communication used, tailoring a message to specific employers means crafting individualized communications that tell them why they can be successful at your institution. "Employers are increasingly looking at other ways to brand themselves to students" (NACE, 2011). Many career centers have created sections of their website designed to help employers increase their visibility and "brand" on the campus. Some examples can be seen at George Washington University (http://gwired.gwu.edu/career/employers/visibility/) and the University of Florida (www.crc.ufl.edu/employers/employerCampusBrand.html). The bottom line is this: (a) create a targeted list of employers that makes sense in regards to your student population, (b) tailor your message to align with the employer's recruiting needs, and (c) use as many media as possible to get the message out (e.g., marketing visits, calls, electronic communications, prospect letters) (Edds, 2008; NACE, 2011). It is the same rationale a career center uses to encourage students when job searching; be strategic in where you send your message and what your message says.

Once employers engage in one of the many recruiting services, relationship management becomes a key element in maintaining their involvement. Regular communication is essential, whether in the form of periodic newsletters, e-mails, "hold the date" postcards (see example in Appendix J), special invitations, or even phone calls about new recruiting opportunities. Employers are seeking schools that can help them achieve the goals of branding their organization to students and identifying talent early (NACE, 2011), as well as those who are willing to customize recruitment services to meet their specific needs. Customer service means anticipating employers' needs, meeting them, and then following up with other services after delivery. Complacency may quickly turn a robust recruiting program into an office with declining employer numbers. Ensuring brand recognition on campus makes the employer relations team an essential partner with employers and increases long-term, win-win relationships for students, employers, and the institution.

Connecting to Administrators, Faculty, and Staff

Another vital stakeholder to a career center's marketing strategy is the university community. Administrators, faculty, and staff are important collaborators and partners for successful career services marketing to students (NACE, 2010). In order to enlist assistance from this group, career services must first market to the university itself. Newsletters, e-mails, and social media are not only ways to inform the university community about career services and upcoming programs and events, but these tools can be used to encourage the institution to promote various events for students and employers. Even with these types of promotions, faculty and staff may not realize how important they can be to a career center's mission and the impact they can have on students and employers. By simply being advocates for career services, administrators, faculty, and staff can increase student interaction and attendance at employer events. Reaching out and marketing to administrators, faculty, and staff requires a willingness to partner, communicate, and collaborate.

One of the ways career services can collaborate with faculty is to offer guest speakers and career-related workshops for their classes. Whether the workshop focuses on a topic of interest or it simply solves professors' problems of having to cancel class when they cannot be present, these types of activities provide a means for employer relations staff to support faculty. This strategy can help career services with its goals of not only becoming better connected to faculty, but it can ultimately help us reach students where they are captive audiences—in the classroom. Another important strategy is to create strong relationships with influential administrators, faculty, and staff in colleges and departments, so career services staff will be included in important planning meetings. If career services staff can be at the table when career programming is discussed, they are more likely to be asked for advice and assistance with any career- and employer-related initiatives. Career services staff need to be viewed as the experts in career programming and event planning for both students and employers in order to enhance high-quality offerings (NACE, 2011).

An effective way to enhance communication and marketing with colleges and departments is by assigning staff to college specific responsibilities. As described in Chapter 2, many career services have identified liaisons for various academic units and departments. An example of this can be found on the Texas State University's website: www.careerservices.txstate.edu/about/collegeliaisons.html. On the lead author's campus, career center staff are assigned as liaisons to colleges and various departments and/or centers. Staff engage in activities, create programs, and develop relationships that not only promote the center's services, but they also help to set a direction for the types of programming that meet the needs of students within that academic unit. Occasionally, liaisons will partner with other university staff in order to create joint programs or events. This type of collaboration not only ensures input from colleges and schools, but it also increases the likelihood of support. Sample activities that might be part of a liaison role include the following:

- Making recommendations regarding career information and/or job search resources that should be maintained by the career center to meet the specific needs of students in a college's various academic programs

- Making sure the school/college gets copies of career center materials (e.g., Career Guides, publicity flyers for career fairs and other events), especially keeping any peer advising office stocked with materials

- Faxing or e-mailing job notices that might be of interest to students to key staff and faculty

- Becoming familiar with the career/academic needs of students enrolled in specific majors within the college and informing/training career advising staff regarding this information

- Developing selected materials, services, or programs (career forums, workshops) to help students identify various career alternatives and job opportunities associated with majors in that college. This could also include revising and updating previously existing career center materials (e.g., informational sheets connecting fields of study to occupations and other career and employment resources related to a particular discipline.) For a comprehensive list, visit http://career.fsu.edu/occupations/matchmajor/.

- Developing links between the career center and college websites that address career information and services specific to the college and its majors

- Recommending website links that relate to the needs of students in a particular college/school

- Attending meetings of academic advisors or faculty and informing the college/school of current career-center services

- Providing career center staff with current information associated with the liaison's respective college/school

- Inviting faculty, advisors, and other staff from the school/college to a career center open house

- Generally serving as a contact and conduit for the exchange of information and referrals between the respective college/school and the career center

- Meeting individually with students from a particular school/college who need more in-depth assistance with their career planning and/or job hunting

When administrators, faculty, and staff believe career services are not just about assisting "students" in being successful, but that they are assisting "their" students in particular, then collaboration and partnerships can be formed that benefit everyone. Developing a strong marketing campaign with faculty, staff, and administrators provides a valuable channel for reaching students, and it also completes the connection between employers and the campus community.

Determining a Cost-effective Marketing Strategy

As previously noted in this chapter, marketing to students, employers, and faculty, staff, and administrators can make the difference in a career services' effectiveness and increase its impact on both clients and the organization. Researching the audience, clearly defining program goals, creating a marketing strategy and activities, and obtaining customer feedback are essential components for successful marketing (Edds, 2008). An easy first step in this process is to develop and maintain a standard list of the center's current publications and promotions. After crafting this list, ask the following questions:

- Who is the target audience for the marketing piece?
- What is the objective?
- Did you tell the targeted audience how the program or service benefits them?
- Is the language relevant and appropriate for the target audience?
- Is the publication and its marketing message clear and easy to read?
- How much does it cost to produce and distribute?
- How often must it be produced?
- Is there a common brand between publications and promotions?
- Is there a more cost-effective method to get the message out?
- How, where, and when will a print publication be distributed?
- Can the cost of the publication be shared with another campus department?
- Should this publication continue to be used?

After answering these questions and revising the publications if necessary, staff can create clear timelines for the distribution and production of these publications and determine the person or persons responsible for both functions. Appendix K provides a publications list, and Appendix L provides a distribution timeline for marketing services and programs to students, employers, faculty, staff, and administrators. Both examples are from the lead author's campus.

With such a vast array of methods and channels for publicizing services and programs, the marketing strategies practitioners chose to employ will ultimately depend upon the office's needs, budget, and available resources. Creating a balance of website applications, publications, publicity/news releases, and social media challenges most career centers. Edds' (2008) NCDA monograph, *How to Market Career Development Programs and Services*, noted that the effective marketing of programs and services relies on three keys: (a) distributing the message in a cost-effective manner, (b) to the right people, (c) at the right time. Without these elements, the entire process can fail. Unfortunately for many practitioners, the key ingredient in this list revolves around the available money and resources that control both the type and amount of marketing materials a career center uses.

Figure 4.3 illustrates some common marketing methods available to career services practitioners. The location of each strategy on the pyramid reflects the amount resources required for their use. Career services offices with limited resources may want to employ the methods at the top of the pyramid as those at the bottom require the greatest investment in time, money, and knowledge. Whichever methods an office adopts for their marketing campaign, it is critical to make sure the following elements are considered when developing the promotional materials (Edds, 2008).

- Who are you; what is your purpose?
- Who is the publication targeting?
- What is the message?
- What is the desired outcome?
- What is the budget?

Answering these questions prior to creating any publication will create a roadmap to guide marketing efforts to successful outcomes.

Figure 4.3. Examples of career services marketing techniques in terms of cost, time, and expertise.

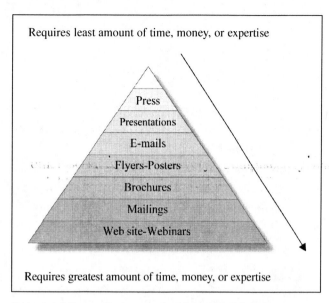

Figure 4.3. From *How to market career development programs and services.* By C. Edds. Copyright 2008 by the National Career Development Association. Reprinted with permission.

Summary

Effective and strategic marketing to all career services' stakeholders is a dynamic and essential target. Employer relations staff and marketing personnel must know their clients, (e.g., students, employers, faculty/administrators) and keep up with the issues and trends that affect them. Creating powerful marketing partnerships by connecting to faculty and administrators requires understanding their goals and priorities and showing them how career services can be pivotal in their students' success. Having a clear message and crafting publications and promotions that send it in a concise and relevant way is a wise investment of time and resources. Continuously investigating new ways of "getting the message out" and collaborating whenever possible saves time and money. Whatever level of funding and staffing is available for this critical role, career services must stay vigilant in pursuing and accomplishing the task of effectively marketing its programs and services. A proven marketing strategy that brands the career center and produces results is required for employer relations to be successful in meeting its goals.

References

Carvalho, S. W., & de Oliveira Mota, M. (2010). The role of trust in creating value and student loyalty in relational exchanges between higher education institutions and their students. *Journal of Marketing for Higher Education, 20*(1), 145–165. doi:10.1080/08841241003788201

Edds, C. A. (2008). *How to market career development programs and services.* Broken Arrow, OK: National Career Development Association.

Giordani, P. (2012, February). Tracking social media effectiveness. *NACE Journal, 72,* 22–25.

Herr, E. L., Heitzmann, D. E., & Rayman, J. R. (2006). *The professional counselor as administrator: Perspectives on leadership and management of counseling services across settings.* Mahwah, NJ: Lawrence Erlbaum Associates.

Kubu, E. (2012, April). Career center social media implementation and best practices: Findings of a nationwide survey. *NACE Journal, 72,* 32–39.

National Association of Colleges and Employers. (2006, October 27). Meeting the challenge: effective marketing to students. *Spotlight Online for Career Services Professionals.* Retrieved from http://www.naceweb.org/knowledge/cs/Marketing_to_Students/

National Association of Colleges and Employers. (2009). *NACE professional standards for college and university career services.* Bethlehem, PA: Author.

National Association of Colleges and Employers. (2010, July 21). Marketing the career center to faculty. *Spotlight Online for Career Services Professionals.* Retrieved fromhttp://www.naceweb.org/Publications/Spotlight_Online/2010/0721/Marketing_the_Career_Center_to_Faculty.aspx

National Association of Colleges and Employers. (2011, April 27). Marketing your school to employers: What employers want. *Spotlight for Career Services Professionals.* Retrieved from http://www.naceweb.org/s04272011/marketing_branding_employers/

National Association of Colleges and Employers. (2012). *NACE 2011–12 Career services benchmark survey for four-year colleges and universities.* Bethlehem, PA: Author.

CHAPTER 5
Information Systems and Technology

Over the last forty years, how employer relations and recruitment services are conducted (e.g., managing employer and student services, creating and developing relationships, communicating information) has dramatically changed because of technology. As Herr, Heitzmann, and Rayman (2006) noted, "Nearly all of the functional units within career services depend heavily on technology for their operation" (p. 156). Since the time of the collection of paper job listings by hand to the use of telephones and word processing and finally to Internet-based career management systems and the vast array of Web 2.0 tools, employer relations and recruitment services staff have been compelled to implement new technology in order to provide more information and services to meet the recruiting and job search needs of students as quickly and efficiently as possible. Small and large career centers alike find that the effective implementation of technology and information systems requires not only time, effort, and resources, it also necessitates constant reviews of the latest products in order to stay up-to-date with the most current service-delivery methods. The extent to which career centers use technology varies within the field and is often a result of the demanding requirements in evaluating and adopting technology, the career center's size, access to technical support, and the financial resources available.

This chapter reviews the types of technology and information systems used by employer relations and recruitment services practitioners to effectively meet the needs of students, alumni, and employers. Additional suggestions are provided related to strategies for evaluating systems, partnering with other campus units, and obtaining funding for software systems. Effectively assessing, implementing, and managing technology and software systems is critical to the future success and impact of a center's employer relations and recruitment program. We begin with a brief discussion of the history of this area, followed by a review of the current career services management systems, ways to partner with this technology, and potential funding sources.

History of Technology in Employer Relations

The earliest recruitment systems can be traced back to the centralized job postings associated with Frank Parsons, who created the Vocations Bureau in 1908 in a settlement house in Boston (Reardon, Lenz, Peterson, & Sampson, 2012). Parsons traveled throughout Boston collecting job notices from shopkeepers and made them available to job seekers in one location. Following this earliest concept of centralizing services, later technology advancements produced systems that provided ease of distribution and access to job opportunities. In the late 1970s and early 1980s, software allowed staff to create spreadsheets of job listings, employer visits, and information sessions, improving the efficiency of compiling this important information. Even with this new technology, the distribution of employment information still required job seekers to visit the office or have listings delivered via mail. During the latter part of this time period, the emergence of the personal computer and telephone job lines allowed career services offices to improve the collection and distribution of job notices. Video conferencing arrived on the heels of voice job lines and was introduced as the system that would change the future of candidate recruiting; however, it was not until the advent of the Internet that the opportunity to provide an array of services dramatically changed how candidates were recruited. E-mails, e-mail lists, websites, videos, and applicant tracking systems are just some of the technical advances that came about because of the Internet and allowed career services professionals to provide instant communication channels and offer 24/7 access to recruitment services. In 2006, it was reported that 1 in 10 employers use social networking websites as part of the hiring process (Giordani, 2006). Facebook, Twitter, Pinterest, and LinkedIn (and, of course, blogs) are some of the media channels that career service professionals use to supplement the technology common in the field. As indicated in Chapter 4, these popular tools require career service professionals, or knowledge experts, to use them strategically to meet the career center's marketing goals. Ensuring that this new web-based technology addresses the needs of employers, students, and alumni is a difficult task, but it is a critical component of the services required in today's employment environment. The next section briefly highlights some of the systems most widely used in support of employer relations.

Current Premier Systems

According to the National Association of Colleges and Employers *2010–11 Career Services Benchmark Survey for Four-Year Colleges and Universities* (NACE, 2012), the most commonly used technologies were website and online job postings, and the most effective were online interview scheduling systems. The least common systems were electronic portfolios and virtual career fairs. Consistent with these results, many career services offices throughout the country use career services management systems such as Experience, Symplicity, CCN, or CSO to provide these services. These systems offer components that support some of the main recruitment services offered by both large and small career centers. Career fair registration and management, on-campus interview scheduling, job listings, résumé books, and employer- and student-database registration and management are core elements found in most of these systems. Purchasing and implementing these systems may increase productivity for the employer relations team, but deciding which system best fits the institution requires careful evaluation (Herr et al., 2006) and consideration of many important factors.

Factors to Consider in Selecting a Recruitment System

Career services management systems can be costly, and adoption clearly depends on the availability of financial resources, the size of the institution, and the desired types of services the employer relations team seeks to offer. Each career services office must not only evaluate the need for this technology, but the office must also determine the breadth of the services to be provided (Venable, 2010). The challenge of determining if a system meets the office's needs should include not just a needs analysis but an effective way to evaluate the technology offered. The first consideration for an employer relations staff in choosing a system may be to ascertain if the technology and the proposed system implementation meet the standards set forth by Council for the Advancement of Standards in Higher Education (CAS, 2012) as shown in table 5.1. The items are rated on a scale ranging from 0 to 5 (including 0 = ND [does not apply]) as follows:

Table 5.1
CAS Standards for Technology and System Implementation

1—unable to rate; insufficient information; 2—does not meet; 3—partly meets, 4—meets; 5—exceeds, exemplary

	Criterion Measures from CAS Standards
10.1	The Career Service (CS) has adequate technology to support its mission and goals
10.2	Use of technology in the CS complies with institutional policies and procedures and legal requirements
10.3	The CS uses current technology to provide updated information regarding mission, location, staffing, programs, services, and official contacts to students and designated clients
10.4	The CS explores use of technology to enhance delivery of programs and services, especially for students at a distance and external constituencies
10.5	The CS uses technology that facilitates learning and development and reflects intended outcomes
10.6	The CS
10.6.1	maintains policies and procedures that address the security, confidentiality, and backup of data, as well as compliance with privacy laws
10.6.2	has plans in place for protecting confidentiality and security of information when using Internet-based technologies
10.6.3	develops plans for replacing and updating existing hardware and software as well as for integrating new technically-based or -supported programs
10.7	Technology selected by the CS addresses distance learners and clients with unique needs and interests
10.8	CS staff are well informed about the array of career-based technological applications
10.9	The CS develops plans for replacing and updating existing hardware and software and for integrating new technically-based or –supported career programs
10.10	Technological applications specific to the CS include
10.10.1	Internet-based resources that provide updated information regarding mission, location, staffing, programs, services available to students and designated clients, and contact information
10.10.2	computer-based assessment and computer-assisted career guidance systems
10.10.3	online recruiting and employment systems that include job listings and student résumés
10.11	Workstations and computer labs maintained by the CS for student use are accessible to all designated clients and meet standards for delivery to persons with disabilities
10.12	The CS provides
10.12.1	access to policies on technology use that are clear, easy to understand, and available to all students
10.12.2	assistance, information, or referral to appropriate support services to those needing help accessing or using technology
10.12.3	instruction or training on how to use technology
10.12.4	information on the legal and ethical implications of misuse as it pertains to intellectual property, harassment, privacy, and social networks
10.13	Student violations of technology are addressed in student disciplinary procedures
10.14	A referral support system is available for students who experience negative emotional or psychological consequences from the use of technology

Copyright 2012 by the Council for the Advancement of Standards in Higher Education. Reproduced by permission.

Another critical aspect of evaluating a career services management system entails determining if the system meets the specific gaps in service delivery while accomplishing the goals of the employer relations team. Employer relations staff may consider other criteria to determine which career services management system meets program needs. Asking the following questions prior to choosing a system can help insure that it incorporates the desired services an office is seeking to offer, with proper cost, reliability, and ease of use.

- What is the annual cost of the system? Who will pay for the system and will this cost be shared?

- How many years has this vendor been providing the service?

- What other career centers, similar in size and services, currently use the system? What do these career services offices say about the system's reliability and the vendor's customer service and responsiveness to issues?

- Does the vendor incorporate new technology into the system in an effective way that does not compromise the functionality of the services being delivered?

- Does the system ensure integrity of both student and employer data?

- Will this system be easy for the employer relations team, students, and employers to use?

- Will staff be initially trained by the vendor and is on-going training included in the service? What level of on-going support will you receive?

- Does the system interface with existing software? Will the system meet not just current needs but also future needs? Is the system customizable to meet your unique needs?

- Will the system track and report the information required by your administrators? Who in your organization will be the key administrator(s) and what training will they need that they currently do not have?

- What additional impact will adopting this technology have on other services?

- What features must the system provide? What features can you live without?

Carefully asking and obtaining answers to these questions will help an office choose a career services management system that matches the organization's needs and goals. Figure 5.2 outlines the current features offered by a selected group of vendors, and may also be useful in answering some of these questions (C. Offield, personal communication, December 27, 2012; K. Selle, personal communication, December 27, 2012; K. Harris, personal communication, January 3, 2013; D. Brumfield, personal communication, January 10, 2013).

Information Systems and Technology

	CCN	CSO	Experience	Symplicity	Must Haves	Costs
Student/Employer Registration	√	√	√	√		
Document Manager	√	√	√	√		
Job Listings	√	√	√	√		
Event Manager	√	√	√	√		
Interview Scheduling	√	√	√	√		
Student Tracking	√	√	√	√		
Employer Tracking	√	√	√	√		
Appointment Scheduling	In development for 2013 release.	√	√	√		
Sign-in Kiosks	√	√	√	√		
Alumni Network/Mentoring	√	√	√	√		
Credentials File Service	Not a dedicated feature – handled through portfolios.	Not a dedicated feature – handled through the student document section.	Not a dedicated feature – handled through the student document section.	√		
Résumé/CV Builder	√	Partnership with RésuméMaker. In development for 2013 release.	√	√		
Résumé Books	√	√	√	√		
Résumé Referrals	√	√	√	√		
Sales/Campaign Manager	Promotional materials provided.	Some functionality. In development for 2013 release.		√		
E-mailing Individual & Mass	√	√	√	√		
Experiential/Co-op Module	Can record & track experiential learning/co-op placements.		In development.	√		
Calendar Integration	In development for 2013 release.	In development for 2013 release.	√	√		
Merchant Services* (Credit card processing)	√	√	√	√		
Authentication Integration (Verification of user)	√	√	√	√		
Faculty/Guest Accounts	In development for 2013 release.			√		
Surveys	√	√	√	√		
Multi-campus Environment (Multiple independent systems using one database)	√		√	√		
Analytics			√	√		
Placement Tracking	√	√	√	√		
Integration with other Software Vendors	√	√	√	√		
Vendors available for Partnership		Going Global; CareerSpots; Internships.com; CPP; Indeed.com	Going Global; Peterson; Salary.com	Going Global; Career Shift; CPP		

*CCN — PayPal   CSO — Authorize.net   Experience — PayPal   Symplicity — Cybersource, Cashnet, Touchnet, PayPal, and Authorize.net

Some of the leading systems partner with other vendors to supplement the services offered. Likewise, many career services offices contract with similar vendors to supplement their main career services management systems; these additional vendors may include companies such as InterviewStream, Interfolio, CareerShift, and Going Global. These additional systems provide technology that can meet a niche in providing recruitment services, including video interviewing, virtual career fairs, credentials file storage, obtaining key corporate contacts, and identifying international opportunities.

Probably one of the most impactful systems implemented in the last decade is the NACElink Network, a national collaborative recruiting network. This network is a suite of web-based recruiting and career services tools used by colleges and employers. The NACElink Network is an alliance among the National Association of Colleges and Employers (http://naceweb.org/), Symplicity Corporation (www.symplicity.com/), and DirectEmployers Association (www.directemployers.org/) that includes more than 700 participating college career centers, more than 3 million active employer contacts, and more than 7.2 million active students and alumni. This partnership emerged out of the need to develop a software system to support job listings, college student résumé databases, and on-campus interviewing/recruitment services that was under the control of the educational institution. Prior to this partnership, private vendors such as MonsterTrak were making profits from graduates and employers and refusing to protect student data. A core group of educational institutions sought to create a system that would give them greater control in protecting student data and in managing the costs associated with these systems.

Florida State University, along with six other prominent institutions with established and highly-regarded career services offices, initiated development of a nonprofit on-line system that could serve as a national recruiting system for colleges and employers. Initially, DirectEmployers (a non-profit organization) and a product development team formed with staff from the initial seven schools and several key employers partnered with NACE to develop the software for a career services management system. Creating the software to drive this system, however, proved to be a monumental task and, ultimately, the Symplicity Corporation was contracted to provide the software infrastructure for the NACElink Network. Eventually, this project came to fruition with 27 nationally prominent career centers partnering with the NACE (the profession's guiding association), DirectEmployers Association, and Symplicity Corporation. Currently, the NACElink Network supports more than 560 schools and nearly half a million employers. While NACElink Network provides the needed one-stop shop for employers to post jobs at multiple institutions, career services still require additional systems to support employers recruiting efforts.

Since the formation of this partnership, Symplicity has become known as one of the flagship career service management systems and has contracted individually with institutions to provide additional services that supplement the NACElink Network. Two other career services management vendors, CSO and Experience, compete in this marketplace by providing a suite of similar services. College Central Network (CCN) also provides a much needed product for smaller institutions that have less robust resources but are seeking many similar features. In today's competitive market of attracting employers to recruit on campus, career services must adopt a career management system in order to be effective in providing opportunities to students (Herr et al., 2006). Whichever career services management system is selected to meet the office's goals and budget, a periodic evaluation of available systems and any additional supporting technology is necessary. Career services and employer relations rely heavily on technology to support recruitment activities that ultimately support students' employment opportunities (NACE, 2012). Figure 5.3 is adapted from results of a NACE survey and shows the varied technologies used by career centers in the U.S.

Figure 5.3. Technologies Employed at Career Centers

	Yes		No	
	# of Respondents	% of Respondents	# of Respondents	% of Respondents
Career Center Website	588	98.5%	9	1.5%
Electronic Portfolio	126	22.2%	442	77.8%
Online Career Counseling	312	54.4%	262	45.6%
Online Interview Scheduling	324	56.0%	255	44.0%
Online Job Posting	576	97.0%	18	3.0%
Online Tutorials	331	57.6%	244	42.4%
Video Interviewing	214	37.7%	354	62.3%
Virtual Career Fairs	107	19.5%	443	80.5%

Figure 5.3. Adapted from *NACE 2011–2012 Benchmark Survey.* Copyright 2012 by the National Association of Colleges and Employers. Reprinted with permission.

Ways to Partner with Technology

Leveraging technology to meet the needs of career services and its constituents is commonplace today and provides a winning solution for institutions in meeting with budget constraints, increasing their return on investment, and creating mechanisms to improve student success (Davidson, 2001; Herr et al., 2006). Partnerships formed between career services and academic colleges/departments to share career management services technology provide an opportunity to implement a system that previously would not have been possible and create an alliance that strengthens the role of careers services within the university community. Some of the most common partnerships to explore when implementing new technology occur with alumni associations and academic colleges and/or departments who have ventured into providing career services.

In recent years, there has been a "surge of support for alumni career services among the nation's colleges and universities" (Herr et al., 2006, p. 168). Many alumni associations know that providing an array of career-related services to their members will not only increase their value to these members, but this value-added service in membership benefits can also serve as an effective recruitment and marketing tool. Likewise, career services can benefit by sharing costs and avoiding duplicate services by implementing joint systems. Colleges and departments can also benefit from the alumni/career services partnerships. Technology that connects alumni to support students' career exploration, experiential education, and future career opportunities can be leveraged to form partnerships with colleges. One common system often shared by career services with these partners is an alumni and job-listing database. By joining efforts and implementing shared systems, institutions can provide a network of resources in a cost-effective, nonduplicative environment. At Florida State University, two examples of successful partnerships that share technology across colleges and departments are the use of an alumni database (ProfessioNole, http://career.fsu.edu/professionole/) and the implementation of a "Multi-School Environment" (i.e., where the career center and an academic department share an employer/student database).

The ProfessioNole program connects students

with professionals throughout the country and world. Students can seek out professionals in their area of interest to learn more about industry demands, career expectations, and current and future employment opportunities. This information database serves dual purposes by providing students' access to alumni and giving alumni an opportunity to give back to the university by sharing their knowledge and experience. Recently, this program was extended to provide a platform for colleges to administer their mentoring programs. For example, FSU's College of Business Student Leadership Council had previously developed a professional mentorship program that required students to apply, be chosen, and then assigned to industry leaders. This process was time consuming and cumbersome. At a liaison meeting with the group advisor, a partnership was formed to conduct the mentorship program through the ProfessioNole system. Both partners stand to gain many benefits from this collaboration. Students and employers only have to register in one system, increasing opportunities for connections. The college benefits by using a system that vets employer/alumni registration and protects student data. Reports can be run on employer and student activity, application and résumés can be submitted, and records of mentor assignments make the system user friendly. This successful collaboration between the career center and an academic unit in leveraging technology has provided a useful template for creating similar programs in other colleges.

Some career services management system allows institutions to purchase a shared system. This "Multi-School Environment" system allows offices who provide separate services and operate independently from each other to share some common data (e.g., students and employers) but retain independent customization and branding. This type of system allows each partner to share jobs, employers and contacts, events, and dual-affiliated students (i.e., students who work with both offices) all at a potential cost savings of thousands of dollars. The greatest benefit, besides cost, is that both employers and students only have to access one system, allowing the login process to require only one unique identifier by the user. Most system settings are unique to the individual school, department, or career services office, except for a set group of settings that must be decided jointly. This customization provides branding of headers and footers, creates specialized forms, announcements, and e-mails, and provides separate web addresses. Initial setup requires strategic planning and effective communication. Identifying a transition leader and holding regular meetings with clear short- and long-term goals are essential to the success of implementing and using this system. Creating a user guide with shared terminology, a FAQ page, and agreed system policies ensure a strong working strategy. Even with strong relationships, effective planning, and shared goals, challenges to effective use are inherent. As with any partnership, varying degrees of commitment and buy-in, knowledge and comfort with the technology, and the amount of time and staff resources committed to the implementation impact the outcome. Reciprocal consideration and compromise for each other are essential components of this partnership.

Funding Sources

Twenty-one percent of respondents in a recent NACE benchmarking survey (2012) have "partnership" programs that generate revenue and support the purchase and implementation of technology for employer relations and recruitment programs (more discussion regarding employer-based partnership funding programs is provided in Chapter 6). Career services can also collaborate with other campus partners to lessen the financial impact of implementing technology. To avoid paying for and implementing unnecessary technology, a needs assessment that reviews program design, mission, available technology, and staffing are essential. Sampson (2008) provided useful guidelines to consider in designing and implementing various aspects of career programs.

Comprehensive systems, or some combination of their components, start as low as several thousand dollars but can easily reach up to $30,000 or more depending on the programs selected to meet the recruiting needs of students and employers. With the majority of career services offices relying on the institution for their operating budget, career services staff must carefully analyze system requirements, costs and benefits, and strengths and weaknesses to ensure that the system or systems chosen can adequately provide appropriate and adequate services. In turn, this type of careful planning can hopefully reduce staff time demands and result in cost savings.

Identifying Alternative Revenue Streams to Support Technology

Increased financial constraints on career services have caused most centers to investigate alternative revenue streams (e.g., student and alumni fees, employer fees). Employer fees continue to be the most common source of this additional revenue and include career fair registration fees, sponsorship programs, and opportunities for advertising to students (NACE, 2012). As noted earlier, the subject of fundraising is discussed in Chapter 6. Most career services offices realize that without the investment in technology, they run the risk of becoming almost obsolete (Herr et al., 2006).

Summary

The impact current technology has on employer relations and recruitment services drives offices to continue to implement systems in order to effectively meet the needs of both students and employers. There are important questions and issues to consider in making decisions about purchasing and implementing technology in support of employment services. While the delivery method has changed over the years, the need to maintain and continue to develop relationships will continue to be crucial in providing effective employer and student services. Career services staff will need to continue to be well informed about the array of career-based technological applications that are in current use and how these can be leveraged to best meet the needs of their key stakeholders.

References

Council for the Advancement of Standards in Higher Education. (2012, August). *CAS self-assessment guide for career services.* Washington, D.C.: Author.

Davidson, M. M. (2001). The computerization of career services: Critical issues to consider. *Journal of Career Development, 27,* 217–228.

Giordani, P. (2006, Fall). Technology influences the profession. *NACE Journal, 67,* 18.

Herr, E. L., Heitzmann, D. E., & Rayman, J. R. (2006). *The professional counselor as administrator: Perspectives and leadership and management in counseling services.* Mahwah, NJ: Lawrence Erlbaum Associates.

National Association of Colleges and Employers. (2012). *2011–12 Career Services Benchmark Survey.* Bethlehem, PA: Author.

Reardon, R. C., Lenz, J. G., Peterson, G. W., & Sampson, J. P., Jr. (2012). *Career development and planning: A comprehensive approach* (4th ed.). Dubuque, IA: Kendall Hunt.

Sampson, J. P., Jr. (2008). *Designing and implementing career programs: A handbook for effective practice.* Broken Arrow: National Career Development Association.

Venable, M. (2010). Using technology to deliver career development services: Supporting today's students in higher education. *The Career Development Quarterly, 59,* 87–96.

CHAPTER 6
Fundraising and Employer Relations

Career services, unlike many student affairs units (Tull & Kuk, 2012), have long been in the business of exploring opportunities for raising funds (Herr, Rayman, & Garis, 1993). There continues to be a need for career services to be proactive and creative in acquiring the necessary funds to develop and deliver comprehensive programs. Career services can no longer rely on institutional-based funds to fully support operating budgets and, in some cases, the salaries of all staff (Herr, Heitzmann, & Rayman, 2006; National Association for Colleges and Employers [NACE], 2012a). In Chapter 2, we included continua of career services in four areas. The fourth area, focused on the Locus of Funding Continuum, is shown in Figure 6.1.

Figure 6.1. Locus of Funding in Career Services Continuum

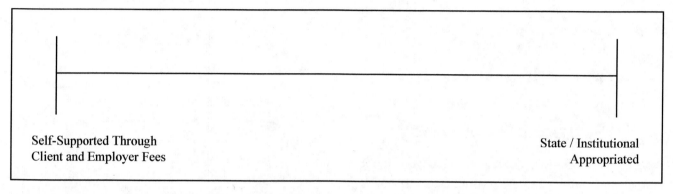

Figure 6.1. Continuum showing the locus of funding sources for career services. Adapted from "Integrating service, teaching, and research in a comprehensive university career center" by S. Vernick, J. Garis, and R. Reardon. Copyright 2000 by *Career Planning and Adult Development Journal, 16,* p. 7–24. Reprinted with permission.

In most cases, the era of career service offices that are fully funded through institutional funds is over, and many offices find themselves in the middle of the above continuum in acquiring funds through a range of sources. Over the years, career service offices have enjoyed an advantage with the opportunity to raise funds through their employer relations programs (Bash & Reardon, 1986). However, as the NACE (2009) professional standards note, "external funding should not be used as a replacement for institutional funds, but can be used to supplement existing budgetary funds in a limited and reasonable manner" (p. 13). This chapter addresses a range of funding sources with particular emphasis on employer fee-based and fund-raising programs. Before addressing these employer-based programs, we briefly discuss other income sources, as well as some important general considerations associated with career services fundraising.

Alternative Funding Sources

Career services should not rely solely on employers as the target of alternative fundraising, and should be creative in identifying a mix of funding opportunities. Herr et al., (2006) discussed a variety of means for supplementing a career services budget. One of the more common funding methods has involved charging student fees for various services; however, there are pros and cons related to this practice (Wendover, 1984). For example, student fees obviously generate added income. Also, in paying for selected career services, it would be expected that students will be more motivated to take advantage of the program, such as participating in on-campus interviewing when paying a recruiting registration fee. Clearly, student fees can represent a barrier for student access and use of career services' programs, and offices should expect to be held more accountable when charging fees. Also, collecting student fees will require additional administrative support and accounting procedures. In our opinion, targeting students for fund-raising through use of specific fees (e.g., a registration fee to access the on-campus recruiting software system) should be avoided where possible. Indeed, many colleges and universities have eliminated student recruiting registration charges in recent years. A recent NACE survey (2012b) found that there was "little fee generation through either student or alumni services" (p. 7). Also, charges for services such as career planning assessments or tests are not recommended.

During tight budget times in years past, it was not uncommon for career services offices to view student fees as a possible revenue stream, including a "fee-based model for career services" (Jones, 2004, p. 28). Some schools have approved and implemented an institutional-wide student fee attached to career services, similar to technology, health, and campus recreation fees. In most cases, these fees have generated considerable income to support career services' programs. For example, an across-the-board technology fee for career services at University of North Carolina (UNC)—Chapel Hill was initiated several years ago and still is in place. At Texas A&M University, all students, undergraduate and graduate, pay a mandatory career services fee of $6.75 per semester to support career services. However, when career services receive student "activity and service" or A&S funds, they are often held accountable via a student governance board regarding budget decisions.

Rather than relying solely on employers or levying student fees, many career service offices have created successful partnerships with other departments and programs to generate funds, (e.g., parents/family associations, alumni associations, academic colleges, departments). Here again, UNC–Chapel Hill serves as an excellent benchmark in creating funding partnerships with the parent/family association. Career services can also be included among donor opportunities through the college or university foundation or development office.

Fund Generation Considerations

Regardless of the array of sources for generating career services' funds, employer-based fund generation is almost always included. An important distinction in funding terms should be made. For the purposes of this chapter, we will refer to "employer fees" paid for career services in support of recruiting efforts while "employer fund-raising" will be associated with donations and contributions to the career services office.

Some student-service professionals may not be comfortable with fund-raising responsibilities (Arminio, Clinton, & Harpster, 2010). Indeed, career services leaders may feel defensive and uncomfortable as if they are begging for employer funds. However, as noted above, most career services offices must engage in charging fees and fund-raising activities to ensure an adequate funding base to deliver comprehensive programs (Herr et al., 2006). Developing clear fee-generation, fund-raising, and budget policies and plans with necessary approvals from appropriate institutional offices will enable career services professionals to feel more secure about having adequate resources to support employer programs and services. Also, from a philosophical perspective, fee-generation and fund-raising activities are ultimately conducted to support the delivery of quality career services to students. Most employers understand and support this as part of their college and university recruitment partnerships. In short, today's career service leaders must embrace and be effective fund-raisers within the context of the employer relations program.

Gaining Institutional Support for Fundraising

Reference was made to obtaining necessary approvals from the institution in support of fund generation. Specifically, career services should obtain approval in setting and changing employer fees, such as career-fair registration or employer-advertising costs, because most colleges and universities have controller-based policies associated with such practices. Also, fund-raising efforts should be coordinated and approved through the institution's foundation or development office. However, in some cases the definition of "fees" or "contributions" can be blurred. For example, some employer-partner programs may require a contribution, but include advantages such as free advertising or waiving the employer career-fair registration fee. In such cases, career services should be certain that the program meets institutional definitions for a contribution or donation. In most cases, employer fees are placed into auxiliary accounts, while contributions or donations are placed into foundation or development accounts to be used as "enhancement funds" rather than supporting the operating budget. Additionally, many employers must follow protocol, often for tax purposes, regarding the distribution of funds as fees or donations.

Employer Relations Fund-Generation Programs

Specific opportunities for employer-generated income and donations are described in this section, with options associated with very basic employer fees and continuing to more sophisticated fundraising programs. In some cases, a career services office may bundle a range of services for a certain fee. Appendix M shows how the Florida State University Career Center created an information sheet to promote this option. Below, we break out examples of selected services that might be included in various employee fee packages.

Employer Fees

Specialized Services. As noted earlier, career services are increasingly funded through auxiliary fees. In many cases, institutions charge career centers for services associated with employer relations and recruiting functions such as employer parking or wireless access. Accordingly, the career office may choose to pass on the institutional cost by charging fees to employers. For example, at many schools, the initial contact and experience when arriving for on-campus interviewing is to pay a parking fee. Recruiters may feel that this is a "nickel and dime" approach, and the practice can be erosive to positive employer relations. It would be a gross understatement to note that solving college and university parking issues is beyond the scope of this chapter! However, career services should be cautious in levying too many service fees on employers. Ultimately, it may be worth positive employer relations if the career office budgets for and pays selected employer-service costs. Specialized costs may be better included in a more general fee such as the employer registration amount charged for career fairs. In short, it may be more conducive for positive employer relations to eliminate specialized employer fees and cover such costs through absorbing them in the budget or covering them in more general fee generation programs (e.g., career fair registration or fund-raising programs such as employer partners).

Advertising. Among the highest employer relations priorities is to support the campus awareness, visibility, and identity of the recruiters' organizations. Of course, this provides career services with fund generation opportunities through offering employers an array of advertisement options. Just a few examples of employer advertising or promotional programs include:

- career guide or book ads (an example of this type of sponsorship can be found at:

www.careers.qut.edu.au/employer/2013%20Advertising%20Price%20List%20Career%20books.pdf)

- ads in other publications, such as newsletters
- career fair sponsorships, such as student directories ads, posters, or event sponsorship
- website ads or acknowledgements
- facility-based recognition or ads via posters, displays, or digital signage

Career Fairs. As noted earlier, not all career services offices control, organize, and sponsor their institutions' career fairs. But when they do, career fairs represent another important income generation option. Occasionally, career fairs are sponsored jointly through career services, academic colleges/departments, and/or student organizations. In these cases, event income may be shared among sponsoring organizations. Indeed, employer-based fees associated with career fairs are perhaps the most significant auxiliary funding source for many career services offices. This is an example of moving from the institutionally-based funded end of the continuum shown earlier to a more self-supported, fee-based funding model. Some career services offices rely fully on employer career-fair registration income for their entire operating budget. Others also fund staff lines using auxiliary or "soft funds" generated by career fairs.

While career fair income represents a wonderful opportunity, career services should be cautious as ebbs and flows in career fair attendance are based on the economy, labor market conditions, and employer recruiting practices. As noted in the recent Collegiate Employment Research Institute survey (CERI, 2012), some employers may choose to have less of a presence on campuses and turn towards virtual tools for talent development. Additionally, when career fair income is serving as the primary operating budget base, college or university administrators and financial officers should always keep in mind the temporal nature of such income. Ideally, any auxiliary generated income should carry over to the next fiscal year but, in some cases, career service offices are asked to return auxiliary balances to central administration at the end of the fiscal year. In any case, career services are likely to continue to "exploit" campus career events as a source of employer fees. Some examples of these events and possible fees are shown below in Figure 6.2.

Figure 6.2. Career Events and Employer Fees

Primary event registration—additional costs may be included in the registration fee for items such as:
- extra tables and/or representatives
- parking
- lunch
- access to interview space during or following the event
- electrical connection, wireless access, shipping, and/or on-site copying

Pre-event advertising/sponsorship:
- student newspaper career fair insert
- campus newspaper career fair ads
- student pre-event career fair preparation program sponsorships
- promotional pre-event videos
- sponsorship/logos/website links on the career fair's student website
- sponsorship of special career fair–related events, such as employer/student receptions

During career fairs some possible advertising/sponsorships include:
- employer spotlight poster sponsors
- employer logos at the career fair entrances and/or student registration stations
- employer sponsorship notation at the booth site
- employer sponsorship of specialty items, such as student volunteer T-shirts or bags
- acknowledgement of employer sponsorship and logo on event electronic signage

Figure 6.2 provides some examples of the variety of employer fees and sponsorships available through career fair participation. These are regarded as career fair–based employer fees and not donations (which are addressed later in this chapter). Regardless, career fair employer sponsorships options represents a tremendous source of career services income while providing employers with a range of opportunities to advertise and promote student interest in their organizations' recruitment activities.

Job or Internship Postings. Some career service offices may have an employer fee attached to institutional-specific job or internship postings. However, a more common model is for a fee to be attached when the employer wants the employment opportunity to be posted at multiple institutions. Often, multiple institutional job postings are made through the school's recruiting program software system vendor, and occasionally income sharing arrangements may exist with colleges/universities and the system vendor.

Space Utilization. While not common, some career services charge employers for on-campus interviewing activity and/or access to scheduling on-campus interview rooms. Employers are accustomed to career fair registration fees due to the considerable overhead costs associated with event planning. However, for obvious reasons, career services should proceed with caution in requiring an employer fee for participation in on-campus interviewing. Also, career services offices should carefully examine additional specialized employer fees (e.g., parking, wireless access), in order to create a welcoming and employer-friendly environment to maximize their on-campus interviewing activity for students. Fees associated with employer information space are more common. These types of fees are typically paid directly to the facility (such as the student union) rather than career services levying and collecting employer fees for access to campus facilities.

Program or Event Sponsorship. Event sponsorship is often a part of career services' employer relations fee generation. Examples include employer sponsorship of business etiquette dinner programs, diverse student employer receptions, and leadership student networking events. The above examples are considered employer fee-based programs with income generally placed into career services' auxiliary accounts. However, as noted earlier, the line is often blurred between employer fees and contributions. Frequently, donation-based employer relations opportunities include or "bundle" selected programs into the contribution package. Some examples of employer fundraising programs are shown in the following section.

Employer Fundraising

Employer Displays. A common and basic approach to employer fundraising is to create vehicles for acknowledging employer donors. For example, many career services acknowledge employer donors through corporate logos on their websites, traditional posters/displays, electronic signage, and publications such as newsletters or annual reports.

Employer Partner, Corporate Affinity Programs. As noted earlier in the chapter, many career services create corporate or employer partner programs that serve as the primary employer relations fundraising activity. Often such programs are based on an annual membership or contribution level. Additionally, employer partner programs can be offered at donation levels such as platinum, gold, and silver levels. It is common for the donation levels to be associated with school colors, mascots, or college/university symbols. Partner donations are commonly placed in foundation or development accounts and used as enhancement funds, and the donations may be acknowledged through display of the corporate/organizational logos on a website and in publications.

Employer partner programs often include other advantages, such as the following:

- Full page color ad in the career guide/book distributed to undergraduate and graduate students
- Acknowledgement in the career guide and career services newsletters
- Placement of an employer display board in the career services' building

- Acknowledgment of employer partner status with the employer logo shown on the career services' building digital or other media signage screens and linked on the career services' website
- Early access to scheduling on-campus interviews
- Opportunities to present at career services' staff meetings and hold "Employer-in-Residence Days" that include class presentations, faculty/staff networking, and offer student services such as résumé reviewing and mock interviewing
- Free employer parking when conducting on-campus interviews

Also, when career services are the principal sponsor of career fairs, employers may receive a registration fee waiver, preferred booth location at career days, acknowledgement of their partner status at the fair (e.g., entrance displays, booth acknowledgment, electronic signage, notation as an employer partner in student career fair employer directories).

Advisory Boards. In some cases, employer partnership also includes membership on a career services advisory board. These advisory boards are described in more detail in Chapter 7. While representing very powerful fundraising opportunities for career services, care must be taken in designing employer partner programs. For example, employer partners may be given a seat on an advisory board, but donor membership should not be a requisite for all board members. When access to career services programs and services is pinned to employer partner status, a potential "slippery slope" is created in limiting employer access to student recruitment activities based on partner membership. In some cases, decentralized academic college-based career offices create partner programs with employer members provided access to their "best and brightest students" or with access to recruiting programs restricted to partner members only. Such employer partner programs represent so called "pay to play" fundraising programs and carry risks of violating ethical standards of professional conduct for career services (NACE, 2009). Many employers also express concerns and may feel that their hand is being forced to recruit students in selected colleges or departments when access is based on partner membership.

Partnering with Other Institutional Development Programs. As noted earlier, career services should be certain that an employer partner program is accepted and seamlessly included in their college or university corporate relations and development program. In some cases, development or corporate relations administrators may express concerns regarding the creation or expansion of corporate affinity programs. When these programs are taken as an institutional-wide aggregate, they may diminish opportunities to build larger more comprehensive corporate relationships and ultimately "leave funds on the table" because recruiters are not incentivized to assist in developing broader relationships. With the above comment noted, employer programs offer great promise as a core career service fund-raising program. An example is provided by the Carnegie Mellon "career partner program," which is described as a means to "recognize employers who support our innovative programs and initiatives and invest in the professional development of our students and alumni" (www.cmu.edu/career/employers/partners/index.html). Another example can be found on the Oregon State University career services website where they highlight the advantages of being an "Orange Circle Sponsor" (http://oregonstate.edu/career/node/119).

Also, some career centers have included a form or "button" on their website that allows donors to give directly to the career center or specific career center initiatives. The Southern Methodist University Career Development Center has a "Make A Gift" option on their home page (http://smu.edu/career/) and the University of Michigan website include options specific to career services (https://leadersandbest.umich.edu/page.aspx?pid=371&s-Tags\Value=dsa-career-highlighted&s-search=1&noPriority=1).

Career Services Facility Room Sponsors. Another common employer relations fund-raising program is to offer career services' rooms for employer naming opportunities (Herr et al., 1993). Here again, career services should ensure that this, or any other fundraising program, receives full institutional support. Consideration should be given to sponsorship time length for named rooms. For example, are named rooms for perpetuity or for defined periods with opportunities for renewals? Of course, decisions must be made regarding available rooms and donation levels for named rooms. Also, concerns regarding use of named rooms by other competing employers have been well chronicled. For example, a very undesirable situation is created when a recruiter for a selected company is assigned to an interview room named by one of their principal competitors! The University of Maryland's University Career Center & The President's Promise program (www.careers.umd.edu/giving/) provides employers with a range of giving opportunities within what is called the Circle of Partners Giving Opportunities, including:

- Naming a room within the Career Center
- Sponsor a career-related event at the university
- Sponsor the Bright Futures: Internship Scholarship Fund

Career Services Naming. Some career services offices, as well as supporting programs and services, are named, while in other cases, the facility/building housing the office is named. Naming can be associated with alumni donors, friends of the college or university, or employers/corporations. In light of the magnitude of naming an entire career services center and/or building, such practices almost always involve the institutional development office with professional fundraisers and senior administrators in partnership with career services' leaders. Naming can be proactive, which often involves institutional staff identifying a donor and receiving funds in advance of designing and constructing a new career services facility, or donors may wish to name an existing career services office, facility, or building. Examples of named career services or buildings are:

- The Wasserman Center for Career Development at New York University (www.nyu.edu/careerdevelopment/)
- Smith Career Center at Bradley University (www.bradley.edu/scc/)
- Michelin Career Center at Clemson University (http://career.clemson.edu/)
- Bank of America Career Services at the Pennsylvania State University (http://studentaffairs.psu.edu/career/)
- Hegi Family Career Development Center at Southern Methodist University (http://smu.edu/career/)
- Toppel Career Center at University of Miami (www.sa.miami.edu/toppel/mainsite)

Unsolicited Donations. Many career services offices are the beneficiary of unsolicited contributions from alumni, friends, previous clients, and employers. Unsolicited employer contributions are always welcome surprises, but they usually result from effective employer relations programs resulting in strong recruiting results at the college or university.

Summary

As career services offices evolve toward becoming more self-supporting through fees and contributions, it is vital to create proactive and systematic fee-generation and fundraising policies and plans including many of the options outlined in this chapter. Furthermore, senior career services administrators must be comfortable in creating and leading fee generation and donor programs. Also, career services staff may have opportunities to partner with professional fundraising staff through their administrative unit (such as student affairs) or with the central college or university development office. While not typical, there are some career services offices that include a dedicated fundraiser on their staff.

Examples of fee or donation levels associated with specific fee-based or fundraising programs have been limited in this chapter because fees and donations are scalable in light of the nature and size of the institution and career services office. Benchmarking with other comparable institutions, as well as information available through professional associations as discussed in Chapter 7, is important in determining fee and donation levels associated with core employer relations funding programs, including employer advertising, career fair employer registration fees, employer partner programs, and named career services rooms.

It is also important to remember that employer relations and recruiting programs have budgets and they must also be fiscally accountable. To that end, career services should consult and partner with employers in developing fee-based and fundraising programs that meet the needs of both parties.

References

Arminio, J., Clinton, L. F., & Harpster, G. (2010). Fundraising for student affairs at comprehensive institutions. *New Directions for Students Services, 2010*(130), 31–45.

Bash, R., & Reardon, R. (1986). Fundraising in career development services. *Journal of Career Development, 12*, 231–239.

Collegiate Employment Research Institute (CERI), Michigan State University. (2012). *Recruiting trends 2012–2013* (42nd ed.). East Lansing, MI: Author.

Herr, E. L., Heitzmann, D. E., & Rayman, J. R. (2006). *The professional counselor as administrator: Perspectives and leadership and management in counseling services.* Mahwah, NJ: Lawrence Erlbaum Associates.

Herr, E. L., Rayman, J. R., & Garis, J. W. (1993). *Handbook for the college and university career center.* Westport, CT: Greenwood Press.

Jones, C. F. (2004, Summer). Building a fee-for-services model for career services. *NACE Journal, 64*, 27–32.

National Association for Colleges and Employers. (2009). *Professional standards for college and university career services.* Bethlehem, PA: Author. Retrieved from http://www.naceweb.org/Knowledge/Career_Services/Assessment/Professional_Standards_for_College__University_Career_Services.aspx

National Association of Colleges and Employers. (2012a, February 29). Securing more resources for your career center. *Spotlight for Career Services Professionals.* Retrieved from http://www.naceweb.org/s02292012/career-center-resources/

National Association for Colleges and Employers. (2012b). *Benchmarking survey 2011–2012.* Bethlehem, PA: Author.

Tull, A., & Kuk, L. (2012). *New realities in the management of student affairs: Emerging specialist roles and structures for changing times.* Sterling, VA: Stylus Publishing, LLC.

Vernick, S., Garis, J. & Reardon, R. (2000). Integrating service, teaching, and research in a comprehensive university career center. *Career Planning and Adult Development Journal, 16*, 7–24.

Wendover, R. (1984, Fall). To charge or not to charge: The pros and cons of fees for career services. *Journal of College Placement, 45*(1), 46–50.

CHAPTER 7
Program Assessment and Evaluation

The importance of program evaluation has been associated with the career development profession from its beginning (Herr, Heitzmann, & Rayman, 2006). In recent years, the importance of creating a systematic program assessment plan including outcome-based evaluation approaches has been well chronicled (Makela & Rooney, 2012; National Association of Colleges and Employers [NACE], 2010). Indeed, almost every professional association conference includes workshops on program evaluation and assessing learning outcomes. As one of career services' core programs, employer relations and recruiting must be included in the mix of assessment and evaluation activities.

The measurement of career services' effectiveness in providing employer relations and recruitment programs should consider minimal to maximal approaches to program evaluation, quantitative and qualitative data collection, and professional association standards associated with program evaluation as outlined by the Council for the Advancement of Standards in Higher Education (CAS, www.cas.edu), the National Career Development Association (NCDA, www.ncda.org), and the National Association of Colleges and Employers (NACE, www.naceweb.org). This chapter includes selected examples of evaluation measures from the authors' universities—Florida State University (FSU) and Pennsylvania State University (Penn State)—as well as examples from other institutions. The chapter begins by discussing a range of options for implementing an evaluation process within an employer relations program.

Minimal to Maximal Approaches to Evaluating Employer Relations Programs

As is often the case in a student services unit, the focus is primarily on delivering services, so evaluation is often not at the forefront of office priorities. One way to begin to engage evaluation tasks is to identify and schedule some basic activities that are easily implemented (minimal approaches) and then devise a schedule and plan for more in-depth evaluation activities (maximal approaches). Table 7.1 highlights examples of minimal to maximal approaches. Each of these approaches is described in more detail in the sections that follow.

Table 7.1. Examples of Minimal to Maximal Approaches for Program Evaluation and Assessment

Minimal approaches:	Maximal approaches:
■ Mission statements	■ Benchmarking
■ Annual reports of events and participation	■ Focus groups
■ Satisfaction data	■ Self-audits
■ Needs-based or nonuser surveys	■ External reviews/consultation visits
■ Graduating student first-destination surveys	■ Empirically-based outcome assessment
	■ Advisory boards

Mission Statements

A career services' office mission statement is perhaps the most fundamental foundation for employer relations program assessment. Because an employer relations and recruitment program is an essential ingredient of most career services, it should be reflected in the office mission statement. An example of Penn State Career Services' mission statement follows:

> *We educate and empower Penn State students and alumni representing all academic programs for professional success, excellence, and leadership.*
>
> *Career Services accomplishes this mission through providing comprehensive, quality and innovative programs offered within a collaborative university-wide system, valuing a supportive and responsive person-centered approach, leveraging the global Penn State network, and creating connections between students and employers.*

This mission addresses core stakeholders: students, alumni, academic programs, and employers. The statement ends with the idea of "creating connections between students and employers." Indeed, as noted in previous chapters, most career service offices have dropped the "placement" term from their title and mission, but creating linkages, contacts, or connections between students and employers remains a core function of career services. As a result, employer relations or recruiting programs should be reflected in the office mission.

Another example of a mission statement is from Miami University in Ohio's Career Services (http://www.units.muohio.edu/careers/mission.shtml):

> Career Services seeks to complement the academic mission of Miami University by educating and empowering students to take ownership of their professional development as lifelong learners and to excel in a global society. Furthermore, Career Services provides programs and services that create opportunities for employers, students, and faculty to engage in mutually beneficial partnerships that meet the needs of an evolving workforce. Career Services provides:
>
> - centralized, comprehensive, and coordinated career development;
> - experiential learning;
> - and employer relations programs through functional liaison teams supporting each academic division.

Some career services offices frame their mission statement as a "statement of purpose." An example of that can be found on the UCLA Career Center's website: http://career.ucla.edu/GeneralInfo/StatementOfPurpose.aspx. An additional point regarding the inclusion of employer relations in a career services' mission statement should be made. As Figure 2.1 in Chapter 2 illustrated, career services offices can be evaluated in terms of their location on three core mission continua: involvement in career development and guidance, involvement in experiential education and internships, and involvement in employer relations. Some stress the importance of comprehensive career services maintaining a balance in these core missions (Herr, et al., 2006).

At some institutions, there may be a heavy emphasis on career guidance and counseling programs and less of a focus on employer relations and recruitment services. It is important that institutions determine what balance is most appropriate for their campus, especially taking into account the views of key stakeholders. This balance is also often influenced by the extent to which a campus has centralized versus decentralized career services. As noted in Chapter 2, on campuses with widely decentralized career services, the institution's central career services office should partner with academic, college-based career programs in creating a hybrid employer relations and recruiting system that is understood by students, employers, and staff. Regardless of mission and program structure, all career services offices, including the employer relations programs, must consider ways to document in quantitative form how they are meeting their mission and accomplishing their goals. The following section addresses quantitative evaluation methods in employer relations and recruitment services.

Annual Reports of Events and Participation

Reporting numbers and annual activity levels for core basic programs is fundamental in the evaluation of employer relations and recruiting programs, which includes tracking and reporting activity levels and trends for selected core "basic indicator" employer relations and recruiting programs. Examples of these core programs include:

- career fairs
- on-campus interviews
- employer information sessions
- job or internship listings
- résumé referrals

Another basis indicator is the employment rates of graduates. Graduate follow-up or destination surveys are addressed in a later section. However, career services can and should report activity levels in support of programs that create linkages or connections between students and employers. Trends for core basic indicators in employer relations and recruiting programs can be provided through histograms showing three year comparative activity levels. Figure 7.1 shows examples from the Florida State University Career Center.

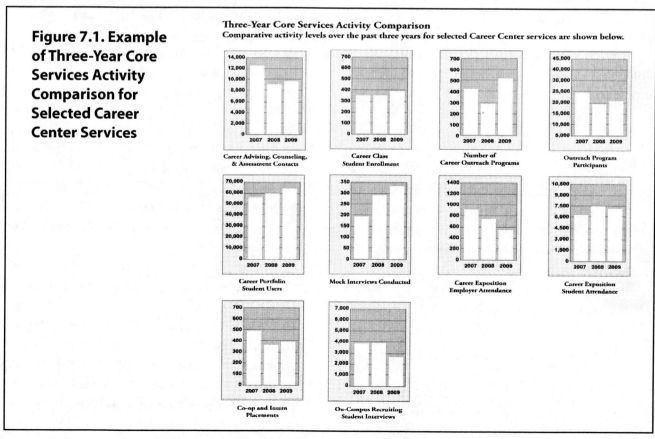

Figure 7.1. Example of Three-Year Core Services Activity Comparison for Selected Career Center Services

Program Assessment and Evaluation

As noted in Chapter 3, the career services office may not sponsor or control all institutional-wide recruiting programs. For example, career services may sponsor and hold some career days, while other career days are conducted by student organizations, departments, and/or academic colleges. In such cases, the career services' annual report may include only career fairs sponsored through its office. However, the career services office can also lead in collecting institutional-wide recruiting data. For example, Table 7.2 shows the Penn State Career Services' 2011–2012 annual report career day activity levels across multiple campus units:

Table 7.2. Penn State Career Services 2011–2012 Annual Report Career Day Activity Levels

Campus Unit	# of Events	# of Organizations	# of Attendees
University Park Career Services Career Days	8	1,349	14,966
University Park–wide Career Days (includes above career services events and academic unit–based programs)	17	1,085	9,130
Commonwealth Campus Career Days	51	2,974	20,305
Penn State University–wide Total Career Days	76	5,308	44,401

Figure 7.2. Top 25 Employers Hiring George Mason University Students, 2010–2011

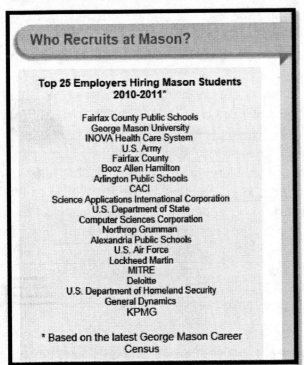

Figure 7.2. George Mason University Career Services Employer Hiring Data found at http://careers.gmu.edu/employers/data/

This activity report in Table 7.2 provides the institution with important university-wide career day information that can be benchmarked with other institutions and serve as a baseline for future trend analysis. Also, the institution, as well as other employers, is typically interested in identifying "top employer" recruiting activity at the respective college or university. Figure 7.2 highlights how George Mason University Career Services presents its list of top employers who hired at that institution during the 2010–2011 academic year.

Such "Top 25" lists of employers by number of interviews conducted and number of hires can also be included in annual reports and other publications targeted to faculty/staff, employers, and other important stakeholders (Sampson, 2008). As noted, quantitative core basic indicator recruiting program activity such as employer career fair registration and on-campus interview activity serve as important barometers for employer relations and recruiting activity at any college or university. This information is typically included in annual reports produced by career services offices.

Most career services offices produce annual reports, both print and web-based, as a requirement of their institutions. Some examples of career services annual reports can be found at the links below:

Florida State University Career Center: http://career.fsu.edu/pubs/Annual%20Report/2011CareerCenterAnnualReport.pdf

Louisiana State University Career Services: http://careercenter.lsu.edu/assessment

Sweet Briar College Career Services: http://sbc.edu/career-services/performance-highlights

University of Florida Career Resource Center: www.crc.ufl.edu/aboutus/AboutReports.html.

University of Iowa: http://www.careers.uiowa.edu/annualreport/

In addition to detailed annual reports or outcome assessments, many career services offices produce a well-designed executive summary that, in addition to career service delivery trends, includes brief snapshots of professional destinations for recent graduates, employer connection programs for students, and recruitment and employment profiles, and which serve as a forum to acknowledge corporate partners. An example from the University of Cincinnati can be found at: www.uc.edu/career/about/annual_exe_summary.html/. In short, with regard to creating linkages between employers and students, the size of the employer relations base matters, and the indicators associated with various employment and related outcomes are key program evaluation measures. We now turn to a discussion of evaluation activities designed to assess user satisfaction.

Satisfaction Data

In addition to collecting program activity data, qualitative user satisfaction surveys serve as a fundamental ingredient in the mix of employer relations program evaluation. In recent years, increased attention has been given to including more maximal or sophisticated evaluation practices, such as the assessment of learning outcomes and evidenced-based practices (Makela & Rooney, 2012). These do not replace the need for minimal evaluation practices such as the gathering of user satisfaction data for recruiting programs such as career fairs and on-campus interviewing. Such data are often collected using Likert scales, but satisfaction surveys may also include open-ended questions in order to obtain general user feedback and comments. NACE (2013) pointed to the need for recruiter data to not only help evaluate the services and facilities, but also to assess the quality of the students and their employment readiness. The Recruiter Evaluation Form used by Bradley University's Smith Career Center is shown in Appendix E. Such user satisfaction survey data can become even more meaningful when combined with benchmarking approaches. For example, a regional group of career centers can create a common recruiter checkout form using a combination of Likert scale satisfaction ratings and open-ended questions. Then each institution can compare their employer ratings with the other universities.

Among the most basic surveys is a simple comment form. The Florida State University Career Center created the form shown in Appendix N. The forms are available in all of the office's public service-delivery areas, including the interview facility. The comment cards can be submitted at any location or placed in a suggestion box at the office's primary entrance. Additionally, the suggestion form is included on the Career Center website (http://career.fsu.edu/forms/comments.cfm) and is available for submission in a virtual suggestion box.

Needs-Based or Nonuser Surveys

Career services staff hear all too frequently student comments like "I've never used the career center" and "I didn't know the career center did that." These types of comments are reported anecdotally and on needs-assessment forms completed by students. Occasionally, it is helpful for the career services office to survey nonusers through creating student survey stations across campus (Harvey & Lenz, 2011). Rayman (2001) discussed the idea of conducting "assessment by walking about" as a way of getting first-hand information from both students and employers regarding their experiences with career services. In surveying random students, we can learn more about their knowledge and use of the career services office while addressing misconceptions. For example, students may note that they have not used the career services office for a reason such as "I thought career fairs were just for business and technical majors." Reardon, Domkowski, and Jackson (1980) used a traverse random sampling technique to assess students' awareness and use of campus career services. In addition, these types of surveys can be done with targeted groups of students (e.g., graduate students, international students, student athletes) on campus to learn more about their unique needs.

Graduating Student First Destination Surveys

As noted earlier, the employment rate of recent graduates is not a complete measure of the effectiveness of career services offices. Obviously, many other factors beyond the control of career services influence employment rates (e.g., global, national, and regional economic/labor market trends, the breadth and quality of academic programs). However, it is still very important for career services to collect and report graduating student destination data. This information can be placed on the career services' website and included in annual reports; moreover, multiple years can be provided to allow for trend analysis and related comparisons. Some examples of this type of data can be found on the following websites:

Florida State University:
http://career.fsu.edu/stats/

Michigan State University:
http://careernetwork.msu.edu/destination-survey-2

University of Missouri:
http://enrollment.missouri.edu/Reports_and_Data/destination_study.php

University of Wisconsin–Green Bay Career Services website:
www.uwgb.edu/careers/connections/graduate-follow-up-survey.asp.

Some schools include a breakdown of student post-graduation data by schools and colleges. An example of this can be seen on the University of California–Berkeley's website: https://career.berkeley.edu/employers/EmpSurvey.stm. Many Australian colleges and universities conduct thorough follow-up surveys (e.g., www.graduatecareers.com.au/research/surveys/). Also NACE offers guidelines for graduate surveys at www.naceweb.org/s08152012/graduate-survey/. A thorough review of the protocol and design of such surveys is well beyond the scope of this chapter. However, a few points associated with graduating student surveys should be noted:

- A reasonable graduate response rate often presents challenges, and career services offices must continue to create systems to ensure a strong response rate or make a graduating student survey an institutional requirement.

- Career services should partner with their division of student affairs, academic colleges/departments, institutional research, and related offices to create a single set of basic post-graduation activity questions. Some colleges and universities create a common set of post-graduation activity questions used across the institution with the opportunity for additional questions to be included by specific academic departments and colleges.

- Most graduating student surveys need a follow-up within 3 to 6 months after graduation to ensure a more complete and accurate picture of students' post-college destinations.

- A first destination survey executive summary can be created for each academic college that includes the following basic information: employment trends, salary data, pursuit of graduate/professional school, representative employers, and representative graduate/professional schools.

Thus far, some minimal approaches to employer evaluation have been described, and the discussion now moves to maximal, advanced approaches.

Benchmarking

Every institution identifies other benchmark schools. Career services can compare employer relations and recruiting program activity through professional association surveys as well as national, regional, and state career services groups. For example, NACE (2012a) conducts and publishes an annual *Career Services Benchmark Survey for Four-Year Colleges and Universities.* In some cases, benchmarking groups are formalized organizations or consortia, while others are regarded as an informal collection of career services directors and/or representatives. Regardless, all benchmark groups offer the opportunity to conduct surveys of recruiting programs, but also offer opportunities for general questions and/or comparisons of employer relations and recruiting practices. Additionally, the career service office may find it advantageous to inform its institution and clients that it is a member of selected benchmarking groups. There are no rankings of career service offices; however, publicizing membership in selected benchmarking organizations and identifying other representative schools can add to office credibility. While career services office accreditation is not a common practice, the Center for Credentialing and Education has an accreditation process for "Centers of Career Development Excellence" (http://www.cce-global.org/CoE).

Some publications conduct surveys and rankings of career services and recruiting programs (e.g., Princeton Review; www.bestcollegesonline.com/blog/2012/07/04/20-colleges-with-the-best-career-services/). In many cases such rankings are fraught with research design, sampling, and validity concerns. However, when the career services office and institution are highly ranked, it can certainly be acknowledged and included in the mix of program evaluation information.

Focus Groups

Conducting focus groups for program evaluation has been a common practice for many years (Krueger & Casey, 2009; Stewart, Shamdasani, & Rook, 2007). Focus groups can be particularly useful when considering a very specific employer relations and recruiting program to meet the needs of a selected student population. For example, a student focus group could be organized to provide feedback and assist in the creation of a new career day targeted to a selected population or career field such as an international career day. An employer focus group was used at Florida State University to learn how employers might respond to and use an ePortfolio system in the recruiting process.

Self-Audits

Most frequently, career services' self audits are based upon professional association standards such as NACE (www.naceweb.org) or CAS (www.cas.edu/). Such audits can be quite time-consuming and require a major staff commitment, but they can be a particularly powerful approach to a maximal program evaluation. Furthermore, the self-audit approach requires staff time and buy-in, but the staff exchange, group dynamics, and feedback can offer numerous advantages. As a result, the self-audit process can be as valuable as the program assessment outcome. The NACE Career Services Professional Outcomes Committee (2007) published a useful resource for this process entitled *Guidelines for Internal and External Review of Career Services*. Also, NACE (2009) publishes a workbook based on its *Professional Standards for College and University Career Services* which includes information on self-audits and provides an excellent tool for a self-audit. Section II of the workbook addresses Program Components, with subsection II-c (items 38–43) focusing on Employment Services. An example Employment Services Program Component is shown below:

41. *Career services must assist students and other designated clients in connecting with employers through campus interviews, job listings, referrals, direct application, networking, publications and information technology.*

1	2	3	N/A Comments	Yes No

Section X of the workbook addresses Employer Relations and Services (items 196–219). An example Employer Relations and Services item follows:

201. *Career services must actively involve employers in on-campus programs that meet career and employment needs of students and other designated clients.*

1	2	3	N/A Comments	Yes No

While self-audits based on professional standards can stand alone as an approach to program evaluation of employer relations and recruiting services, they are often used as a foundation in preparation for an external review of career services.

External Reviews/ Consultation Visits

Although expensive and time-consuming, external reviews are among the most effective maximal approaches to program evaluation. Typically, external reviews focus on the entire career services office, but they almost always include a careful review of employer relations and recruiting programs. Often, external reviews examine the "balance" of the career service office mission for core programs such as career guidance, experiential education, and employer relations (see Figure 2.1) as discussed earlier. Additionally, a major focus of external reviews is frequently associated with the centralization/decentralization continuum for employer relations (see more detail in Chapter 2). Reviews may be conducted solely by external consultants selected by the institution. Consultants may be career services professionals from other benchmark peer institutions or individuals who are regarded as national experts in examining models of career services delivery.

Employers are occasionally included as a member on the external review consulting team. Some reviews are regarded as external/internal when the review team includes a mix of external consultants with internal members of the institution including faculty, staff, and/or students. An external review can be arranged through NACE, as the association offers training for consultants based on its professional standards, evaluation workbook, and the review guidelines noted earlier. For more information on NACE external reviews, visit: www.naceweb.org/career_services/external_reviewers/?referal=connections&menuID=387&nodetype=4

Reviews are most often regarded as proactive because many institutions have a system that routinely requires a periodic review of student service offices, including career services every few years. In some cases, a review may be more reactive and be requested by the institution due to changes in staffing (such as the loss of the director) or perceived concerns regarding the structure or model for the institutional-wide delivery of career services (Rayman, 2001). The *Guidelines for Internal and External Review of Career Services* (NACE Professional Outcomes Committee, 2007) provide detailed information on the components of the review process. Essentially, the review includes preparation with many sample documents such as annual reports, a self-audit, and creation of the review itinerary. The review itinerary typically includes meetings with:

- Career services staff
- Administrators leading the unit to which career services report
- Peer offices within the career services' unit
- Administrators, faculty, and staff representing academic departments and colleges
- Academic advisors
- Other offices such as alumni association, enrollment management, graduate programs, etc.
- Students

A typical external review report may include the following sections:

- Preface
- Mission
- Impressions
- Limitations and Strengths
- Recommendations
- Conclusion

Career services offices that maintain detailed records and summary data as part of their annual reporting will be in a better position to engage in a strategic review process. In addition, these reviews may reveal areas where more complete documentation needs to be maintained in order to ensure that the career services office is living up to its mission and stated objectives. Beyond surveys, annual reports, reviews, and similar data sources, some offices engage in more sophisticated outcomes research, an area that has received more attention in both student affairs and career services in recent years.

Empirically-Based Outcome Assessment

In recent years, and with good reason, more career services offices have sought to engage in outcome-based program evaluation (Makela & Rooney, 2012; NACE, 2013; Rayman 2001). This type of evaluation supports evidenced-based practice through the assessment of learning outcomes. NCDA's (2009) *Career Counseling Competencies* include Research/Evaluation among the minimum competency statements. Also, The *Guidelines for Internal and External Review of Career Services* (NACE Professional Outcomes Committee, 2007) noted:

> ***Student Learning Outcomes*** *— Career services offices are providers of career education and job-search skills. Therefore, it is necessary to demonstrate that the clients are learning something. Assessing student learning is a critical component of the contemporary career services office.*

*Measure of Student Success —
Measuring the success of students in obtaining jobs, internships, externships, interviews, graduate school admissions, and/or defining career objectives is a critical task to demonstrate the definitive worth of the career services office.*

Such outcome-based assessment can vary in its level of sophistication depending on the nature of the program and the resources available to support this type of assessment. In designing a comprehensive career assessment plan, learning outcomes assessment should be included in the mix of evaluation for employer relations and recruiting programs along with the basic evaluation approaches discussed earlier (Makela & Rooney, 2012; NACE, 2013). Career service offices can be strategic in designing an evaluation for a selected outcome. Makela and Rooney (2012) provide an example of how learning outcomes could be assessed for drop-in resume review services. Career services can also partner with faculty and graduate students involved in research that includes assessing program outcomes. For example, Folsom and Reardon (2000) assessed the outcomes of a university credit career development course and found that it had a positive effect on retention for women and diverse students. Career services should take advantage of these partnership opportunities to examine outcomes associated with student involvement in various programs.

Advisory Boards

Advisory boards were addressed in Chapter 6 and also should be included in the mix of employer relations and recruiting program evaluation. Rather than serving as figureheads, advisory boards can be applied working groups serving as a vehicle for meaningful feedback regarding program evaluation (Lenz, 2007; Rayman, 2001). Advisory boards can include varied representation; however, membership at both Florida State University and Penn State include a blend of employers, faculty/staff, and students. The Florida State University Career Center Advisory Committee's mission is:

The Career Center Advisory Committee composed of students, faculty/staff members, and employers assists the Director in strategic program development, evaluation, and planning.

A similar Advisory Board was created at Penn State University, and employer members of the Board were formally surveyed regarding feedback for the design of the next year's career day program with attention to date selection, student participation, and employer registration fee structure.

NACE (2012b) offers guidelines for creating advisory boards at www.naceweb.org/s10102012/career-center-advisory-board/. The NACE Knowledge Center included information about this topic from Jane Linnenburger, executive director of the Bradley University Smith Career Center:

*Choose board members wisely —
Select and invite board members who have experience working with your career center and who offer a range of positions and perspectives. Not only is this range of perspective invaluable to the career center, it's invaluable to the other board members as well.*

*Create value for the board member
— Board members appreciate thoughtful and relevant agendas for on-campus meetings that equip them with information to take back to their own organizations. Don't just ask them to provide you with feedback, but provide them with information—perhaps about new academic programs or insight into student preferences—to help them do their jobs better.*

Connect the board members to students — When the board members come to campus, hold events with them and students. This could include mock interviews and résumé critiques.

Summary

The need for assessment and evaluation of employer relations and recruiting programs is critical to demonstrate a program's impact, inform stakeholders, and document successful outcomes. As outlined in this chapter, program assessment and evaluation can include a range of approaches. Career services offices are encouraged to be proactive in planning a mix of evaluation methods that demonstrate effectiveness in the design and delivery of employer relations and recruiting programs (NACE, 2013). There will be an ongoing need for career services offices to collect data on core employer relations programs and services that show the numbers associated with the scope of employer recruiting activity, student/employer connections, and user satisfaction data. In addition, the evaluation blend should include some selected maximal approaches addressing evidence-based practice and learning outcomes, benchmarking, and/or advisory boards.

References

Folsom, B., & Reardon, R. C. (2000) *The effects of college career development courses on learner outputs and outcomes* (Technical Report No. 26). Tallahassee, FL: Florida State University.

Harvey, E., & Lenz, J. (2011, Fall). *Florida State University career center survey: Executive summary*. Unpublished manuscript. Tallahassee, FL: Florida State University.

Herr, E. L., Heitzmann, D. E., & Rayman, J. R. (2006). *The professional counselor as administrator: Perspectives on leadership and management of counseling services across settings*. Mahwah, NJ: Lawrence Erlbaum Associates.

Krueger, R. A., & Casey, M. A. (2009). *Focus groups: A practical guide for applied research* (4th ed.). Thousand Oaks, CA: SAGE Publications, Inc.

Lenz, J. G. (2007). Career center advisory committees: Connecting with your stakeholders. NCDA's *Career Convergence* online magazine. Retrieved from http://ncda.org/aws/NCDA/pt/sd/news_article/5364/_self/layout_ccmsearch/false

Makela, J. P., & Rooney, G. S. (2012). *Learning outcomes assessment step-by-step: Enhancing evidence-based practice in career services*. Broken Arrow, OK: National Career Development Association.

National Association of Colleges and Employers. (2009). *Professional standards for college and university career services: Evaluation workbook*. Bethlehem, PA: Author.

National Association of Colleges and Employers. (2010, June 9) Key aspects of successful career center assessment. *Spotlight Online for Career Services Professionals*. Retrieved from http://www.naceweb.org/SO/2010/0609/assessment/

National Association of Colleges and Employers. (2012a). *NACE 2011–12 Career services benchmark survey for four-year colleges and universities*. Bethlehem, PA: Author.

National Association of Colleges and Employers. (2012b, October 10) Tips for creating and leading advisory boards. *Spotlight for Career Services Professionals*. Retrieved from www.naceweb.org/s10102012/career-center-advisory-board/.

National Association of Colleges and Employers. (2013, March 20). How to assess your career center. *Spotlight for Career Services Professionals*. Retrieved from http://www.naceweb.org/s03202013/career-center-assessment.aspx

National Association of Colleges and Employers Professional Outcomes Committee. (2007). *Guidelines for internal and external review of career services*. Bethlehem, PA: Author.

National Career Development Association. (2009). *Career counseling competencies*. Broken Arrow, OK: Author.

Rayman, J. R. (2001). Assessing career services. In J. H. Schuh & M. L. Upcraft (Eds.). *Assessment practice in student affairs: An applications manual* (pp. 365–389). San Francisco: Jossey-Bass.

Reardon, R. C., Domkowski, D., & Jackson, E. (1980). Career center evaluation methods: A case study. *Vocational Guidance Quarterly, 29*, 150–158.

Sampson, J. P., Jr. (2008). *Designing and implementing career programs: A handbook for effective practice*. Broken Arrow, OK: NCDA.

Stewart, D. W., Shamdasani, P. N., & Rook, D. (2007). *Focus groups: Theory and practice* (2nd ed.). Thousand Oaks: CA: Sage Publications, Inc.

CHAPTER 8
Future Issues and Trends

The prior monograph chapters provided some insights into future issues and trends in the field of employer relations. This chapter summarizes those topics, calling attention to timely information for readers' future discussion and exploration. Topics covered include accountability demands, continuing issues related to decentralization, fundraising, internships, special populations, recruiting trends such as "just-in-time" recruiting, and third party vendors, and also virtual technology/social media.

Accountability

What is old is new. The monograph authors, who collectively have logged more than 90 years in the field, can remember the dreaded question associated with employer relations—how many students did you "place" this year? As was noted in Chapter 1, the field's history traces how what were once called placement offices have evolved into comprehensive career services centers (Herr, Heitzmann, & Rayman, 2006; Rayman, 1993). Despite this evolution, the enduring question of how successful career services offices are in enabling students to obtain relevant employment continues to be on the forefront of a center's accountability concerns. A NACE (National Association of Colleges and Employers [NACE], 2005) article stated the following: "If one were to point to just one critical issue for career services, accountability would be it" (p. 28). Eight years later, this reality has not changed, but only increased.

As U.S. colleges and universities (as well as many overseas schools) have raised their tuition to replace shrinking government funding, key shareholders, from parents to legislators to students themselves, have treated employment as one measure of a family's return on investment (ROI) of their tuition dollars. Accountability in the past was most often measured in the form of how many students were "placed." Efforts to collect this type of information were, in most cases, woefully inadequate, due to low student response rates and the difficulty in maintaining contact with graduates after they leave the institution, especially at large schools with thousands of graduates. New technology, better tracking by institutions and alumni associations, and social media sites have increased the ability of schools to provide more complete data on the destinations of graduates.

While the terminology has changed slightly, accountability expectations about the employment of students following degree completion have not changed. There is, and will continue to be, a significant focus on data about the job market success of graduating students. Schools are continuing to explore ways to get the highest return rate on follow-up or destination surveys. Online surveys are notorious for their low return rates, which has led some schools to mandate student completion of follow-up surveys. These are often tied to the graduation process in some way, either when students check their final requirements for graduation or when they proceed through the actual graduation ceremony. Regardless of the process used for collecting these types of data, employer relations staff members will need to continue to find ways to lead this effort and make this information readily available to stakeholders requesting it.

We have learned that it is better to "drive" the process and shape the conversation than to have it mandated from above. The role career and employment services staff can play is providing a "bigger picture" response than the simple one related to "did this student, in this major, get placed in a job related to his or her field of study?" It is has always been difficult to assess the criteria "related to field of study" and, in today's changing and diverse global economy, it is even more so. For example, if an anthropology major gets hired by a real estate company, the natural tendency might be to say that the student is not working in his or her field of study. On the other hand, if the student helps the real estate company assess the historical and cultural value of sensitive land tracts prior to construction and land sales, the connection is more easily seen. Regardless of the opportunities that students seek and obtain following the completion of their education, career services must accept the fact that accountability data will be an ongoing demand from various stakeholders, and it is critical that career services has a plan in place to ensure graduate destination data is routinely collected and readily available.

Finally, for many years, there has been discussion of the skills valued by employers (Friedman, 2013, NACE, 2011b). This has led some schools to help students focus on not simply marketing their degree, but the skill set that they have developed over the course of their studies. Schools have developed e-portfolios (Garis & Dalton, 2007; Reardon & Lumsden, 2003) to provide a mechanism for students to showcase skills that they have gained through a wide range of experiences, including internships, volunteer work, on- and off-campus activities, etc. In an age where students are experiencing what some call the "four-year career" (Kamenetz, 2012), students' various life destinations will depend on all of the skills, knowledge, and life experiences they bring to the job market, not just a collection of credit hours from a set of courses.

Decentralization in Career Services

For many years, there have been issues associated with the extent to which career services, in particular employer relations and recruitment activities, occur separate from a centralized career center. Various authors have outlined various the pros and cons related to centralized versus decentralized career services (Herr et al., 2006; Herr, Rayman, & Garis, 1993). Figure 2.1 presented a continuum that showed a completely centralized, comprehensive center at one end and a decentralized center at the other end where responsibilities for career services was found throughout an institution. These services included employment assistance usually housed in academic units or departments. Trends continue to point to the fact that some measure of decentralized career services (particularly employment recruiting programs) will be the norm rather than an exception. Ideally, the college- or university-wide career center takes the lead in creating a "hybrid model" for recruiting services that is understood by students and employers, and provides effective and efficient recruiting services, without duplication of efforts. Regardless of the degree of decentralization, for career services to continue to be relevant and add value to our institutions, we need to take the lead in shaping employer relations/recruiting systems even if we do not fully control them (Garis, in press).

Fundraising

Career services offices, whether in public or private institutions, will need to continue efforts seeking external funding from key stakeholders, especially employing organizations. A key benchmark for any career services office is its strategy for soliciting funds from employers, requesting them to become "partners" with the career center (Bash & Reardon, 1986). While relationships have traditionally been a critical part of soliciting funds for employers, some career services offices have opted to include a "donate" button right on their website. Regardless of the varied methods used for soliciting external funds, employer relations staff must work closely with the career center director and other campus partners (e.g., development office) to find creative ways for obtaining additional funding.

Internships

While internships have a long tradition in career services, the evidence continues to show that reaching out to employers for these types of opportunities is essential to the success of college graduates and their future full-time employment (Collegiate Employment Research Institute [CERI], 2012; NACE, 2011a). Campus follow-up surveys continue to support the idea that students often find permanent employment through their internships (CERI, 2012; Koc, 2010). One employing organization (NACE, 2010) noted that having interns and rotating them through the organization was a more successful recruitment strategy than seeking experienced candidates from outside the organization. The Collegiate Employment Research Institute (CERI, 2012) surveyed employers and found that the "primary purpose for internship and co-op programs is to identify and develop talent for full-time employment" (p. 33). Similarly, employers responding to NACE's *2011 Internship & Co-op Survey* (NACE, 2011a) indicated that approximately 40% of their new hires will be recruited from their internship and co-op programs. The survey noted that increases in internships were "expected in every region and virtually all industry sections for which there are data" (p. 2).

As noted in Chapter 2, institutional responsibility for internships and related experiential education experiences may rest primarily with the career center or may be housed in a variety of campus academic units and programs. For example, at Florida State University, even the International Programs office is involved in providing internship opportunities (e.g., http://international.fsu.edu/Types/Internships/Internship.aspx) along with more familiar academic units (e.g., communications, criminology, education, social work). Regardless of how decentralized internships and experiential education programs may be, career services staff should actively partner with campus groups and departments to ensure students' access to these types of opportunities. One way to do this is to create a campus-wide "internship portal" that includes not only the primary internship office, but directs students to a variety of resources for internships, and even provides information for employers seeking interns. An example of this can be seen at: http://internships.fsu.edu.

A topic that has been the focus of discussions in both the popular media and within career services is the issue of paid versus unpaid internships. NACE (2010) reported that the majority of employer respondents indicated that they paid their interns. Other surveys (CERI, 2012) found mixed results, with the majority of organizations offering paid internships, but this often varies by the type of organization and industry. One trend that has seen more discussion lately is how schools can find resources to support students who are faced with few paid opportunities. A recent e-mail list collected data on the variety of methods that schools were using to attract funds for this purpose. At a time when students are burdened with significant college debt, many career services offices are seeking to find ways to "endow" or fund student internships. For example, NYU's career center created a program (www.nyu.edu/careerdevelopment/funded_internship.php) to provide internship awards, particularly designed to support students seeking internships in settings where there are less likely to be paid opportunities, (e.g., nonprofits). This will be an interesting trend to follow in future follow-up surveys.

Special Populations

One of the many challenges that career and employment services will continue to face is how to best meet the needs of diverse campus groups (Herr et al., 2006; NACE, 2012a). This is particularly true when it comes to employment. Every career services person has heard questions similar to the following:

- What employers will hire people with my major?

- Can I get a job in the U.S. as an international student?

- I am an alumnus and just lost my job … can you help me?

- I am a veteran transitioning back into the workforce … are there opportunities for me?

In the employer relations area, there is an ongoing focus on helping employers connect with diverse student groups. Collins (2011) noted the importance of placing more emphasis on reaching out to specific student groups and using smaller events that bring together employers and targeted student populations. This connection may happen through targeted events, connecting with student organizations or cultural centers on campus, placing ads in publications targeted at diverse student populations, and connecting with faculty and staff who work with campus multicultural programs. Employer handbooks also include sections on how to reach selected student groups through student organization and faculty contacts.

Entire chapters could be written about how employer relations and recruitment services could best serve selected student populations, including students with disabilities, students of color, adult learners, graduate students, LGBT students, and related groups. Many career center websites provide lists of employment resources and websites targeted to diverse student groups (e.g., http://careers.washington.edu/Resources/Diversity-Resources). Other more comprehensive career development texts include content related to this topic (see Niles & Harris-Bowlsbey, 2009; Zunker, 2011). In addition, it is essential that career services help students learn strategies for employment success in increasingly diverse work environments (Andersen & Vandehey, 2012; Reardon, Lenz, Peterson, & Sampson, 2012). The next sections highlight four selected populations that will be the focus of ongoing activity in the employer relations area.

Alumni

Working with alumni is an area that touches all aspects of career services, including employer relations. Forging effective relationships with alumni is a goal of all higher education institutions. Career services have long connected with alumni through networking programs. Earlier, we shared information about how Florida State University has used its "ProfessioNole" (http://career.fsu.edu/professionole/) program to make a connection with alumni and other "friends" of the career center. While alumni often give back in various ways, they are also a target group for services.

Alumni may need services such as career counseling around career transitions; however, they often contact career services in search of employment opportunities due to voluntary or involuntary career changes. There is often a spike in these types of contacts when dramatic events occur (e.g., national crises, 9/11, recessions, global downsizing). The first place alumni often turn when seeking to change careers or seeking employment after losing their jobs is their former campus career center. In light of this, many career services offices have recognized that they need a person who dedicates time to providing alumni with career services. Some schools have long had a career services outreach to alumni. One example of this is "Texas Exes" (http://texasexes.org/career/). This group has been in existence for more than 125 years and, while it provides a diverse array of activities and resources in support of its overall mission, it offers a variety of career services, including career coaching and consultation, mock interviews, and a four-part webinar series related to all aspects of the job search process.

Central to an employer relations program's success with alumni outreach is including all the key stakeholders in the conversations (e.g., alumni association, development office, other key administration officials connected to this area). Also, career services office liaisons may connect to specific alumni groups within various academic units. When employing organizations are targeting alumni for open positions, career center liaisons can make those connections within academic units. It is not unusual to find that academic units have created their own alumni virtual communities using social media platforms (e.g., LinkedIn). Alumni associations are also using social media sites to help alumni connect and tell their success stories (e.g., http://pinterest.com/calaggiealumni/uc-davis-alumni/). Employer relations staff will want to make it a point to connect with these groups so they can be a conduit for employment, internship, shadowing, and related opportunities.

Distance Learners

Career centers continue to explore ways to offer services to distance students (Miller, 2012), but there are unique challenges associated with providing a full range of services to this group, including access to employment services. The increase in distance learners in higher education has been clearly documented over the past few years (Allen & Seaman, 2012). In the period from 2002 to 2010, the number of online students has grown from 1.6 million to more than 6.1 million (Allen & Seaman, 2012). Colleges and universities have continued to grapple with how to best provide student services in general, and career and employment services in particular, to this population. This is particularly true at institutions where the majority of students are online learners (Venable, 2011). Given that their tuition costs may be the same or higher as residential students, online or distance learners may expect career and employment services comparable to those found in brick and mortar settings.

Technology has greatly increased the ability of career centers and employer relations units to provide services, including access to job listings, mock interviews via Skype, networking contacts, and employer contacts via databases, electronic business cards, virtual career fairs, and related tools. Job search counseling and résumé reviews can be provided via online chat services and programs such as Screenr that use screen capture technology and video feedback to allow for distance résumé critiques. Some career services offices have made it a point to address the needs of online or distance learner students directly on their websites. For example, the University of Montana (http://life.umt.edu/career/OnlineStudents/default.php) and Texas Woman's University, (www.twu.edu/career-services/distance-learners.asp) have programs in this area. This use of technology also brings with it a variety of ethical concerns about storage of information, protecting confidentiality, and related topics (Osborn, Dikel, Sampson, & Harris-Bowlsbey, 2011; Sampson, 2012). Even though the precise numbers of distance or online learners will ebb and flow, anyone designing comprehensive career and employment services will need to consider how programs and resources can be extended to this group.

International Students

Surveys (CERI, 2012; Institute of International Education, 2009) have noted the trend of increasing numbers of international students seeking employment assistance from career services offices. For employer relations staff, this means understanding regulations and laws associated with international student employment in the U.S. An important topic in this area is how visa status might affect a student's employment options. As some have reported (CERI, 2012; Dine & Bapat, 2007), employers are reluctant to hire international students due to a variety of factors including language issues, lack of acculturation, "return on investment" (CERI, 2012, p. 38), and the cost and paperwork that may be associated with these hires. Furthermore, in a depressed job market, employers may believe that the higher priority is to hire American undergraduates and graduates.

International students want to know which employers are viable options for them if they are using on-campus recruiting or attending career expos. At schools where the tuition for international students is extraordinarily high, some students may have the expectation that the school will engage in employer development activities on a global scale. Employer relations staff may have to weigh the time spent on this type of outreach versus conducting employer development activities closer to home. Other decisions may involve the extent to which specialized workshops (e.g., helping international students with U.S.-style interviews) are offered (Behrens, 2009). NACE (2012b) provides some guidelines related to best practice for career services staff in advising international students including sharing information about "the reality of the available job market in the United States" (www.naceweb.org/principles/guide/).

Finally, if there is an international student center on campus, their staff and advisors can be helpful in explaining the various work options for international students. As Salmon (2007) noted, "These advisor contacts are the essential sources of information on legal requirements, restrictions, obligations, and opportunities for students and their families" (p. 9). The monograph authors have found it helpful to reach out to international student advisors and invite them to the career center to do an in-service training session for employer relations and any interested career services staff. In addition, a review of U.S. government sites (such as www.uscis.gov) can provide some basic information for staff. Some institutions provide detailed employment resources for international students on their websites. An example can be found on St. Lawrence University's career services page (www.stlawu.edu/studentlife/departments/career-services/page/260). Given that significant numbers of international students will likely continue to seek educational opportunities beyond their home nation and invest significant financial resources to complete their degree, career services staff must find ways to stay current with how employment services can support their job search efforts.

Veterans

The statistics on military service members and veterans enrolling in higher education indicate that the numbers range in the hundreds of thousands and that these numbers are likely to grow, especially as these individuals access the new Post-9/11 GI benefit (National Center for Education Statistics, 2011). While veterans are seeking new educational opportunities, they will also want to know how they can use new and past training in future employment. Supporting veterans in their search for employment has been and will continue to be a topic of interest among career center staff members and recruiting organizations (Bullock, Braud, Andrews, & Phillips, 2009; Giordani, 2012a; Kleinman, 2012). In collaborating with employers who want to reach out to veterans, career services staff will find NCDA's monograph on veterans (Stein-McCormick, Osborn, Hayden, & Van Hoose, 2013) a useful information source on the career and employment needs of this group, as well as various resources available on the U.S. government veterans employment website (www.mynextmove.org/vets/). Employers can also be directed to resources available on the U.S. Department of Labor website (www.dol.gov/vets/). Some career services offices have sections of their website focused on "job search resources for student veterans." An example of this can be seen on Portland State University's website: www.pdx.edu/careers/job-search-resources-veterans. Career center promotional materials can be adapted and targeted to student veterans. An example of this is provided in Appendix O.

Some employers have taken very visible steps to reach out to student veteran populations. On the lead author's campus, staff found significant interest among employers in participating in a "veterans networking night." Employers were not only eager to attend, they were willing to contribute financially to support the event. Employer relations staff can work with their campus veterans' liaison to learn how to best market the skills of veterans to prospective employers. Workshops that help veterans effectively translate military skills to civilian résumés and promote these skills in an interview will be a key aspect of future programmatic offerings comprising student veteran job-search support.

Recruiting Trends

Many predictions continue to be made about what form college recruiting will take in the future (CERI, 2012; Dey & Real, 2010). We have watched over the years as discussions have occurred about the outsourcing of collegiate recruiting—why not just hire an outside firm to match employers with students? As we have stressed throughout this publication, this type of mindset ignores the field's knowledge base, professional standards, and principles. It is incumbent upon employer relations and career services staff members to educate administrators, legislators, and other stakeholders about how turning this service over to outside groups does a disservice to the standards and principles that guide employer relations programs.

One of the most common trends in this area is the rise of "third party recruiters," discussed earlier in Chapter 3. A review of the NACE website, www.naceweb.org, reveals many publications related to this topic, (e.g., *A Student's Guide to Interviewing with Third-Party Recruiters,* NACE, 2006; *Principles for Third-Party Recruiters,* NACE, 2012b). These principles of are designed to help "career services ... make appropriate decisions about the use of these third-party, contractual, and staff services in their operations, including career fairs" (NACE, 2012b, p. 6).

Many career centers publish policies and guidelines related to this issue directly on their website. Some examples of these include one from Bowling Green University (www.bgsu.edu/offices/career/page74889.html) and another from Kansas State University (www.k-state.edu/ces/employers/thirdpartyrecruiters.html). Third party recruiting is unlikely to disappear from recruiting practices, which suggests that employer relations staff must learn the facts about this topic and stay knowledgeable about best principles and practices. In addition to consulting relevant professional associations, employer relations staffs should consult with their own institutional legal team about any other issues related to this practice that may impact students in a negative way.

Another topic of discussion related to recruiting has to do with the prediction that employers will be less likely to visit campuses, participate in one-on-one interviews, and campus career fairs (CERI, 2012; Smith, 2012). In this age of technology and social media, employers seeking talent have many ways to do that which do not involve traveling to college and university campuses and conducting face-to-face interviews. The authors remember many years ago when the prediction was made that videoconferencing would be the "death" of on-campus interviewing. While this prediction has not come true, there is no denying the fact that employers will take advantage of any resource or technology (CERI, 2012) that allows them to find the talent they need, while minimizing costs to locate that talent. Employers recognize the significant costs associated with hiring the wrong people (Bolles, 2013). While the overall numbers of employers visiting campus may decline in some areas, employers in one recent survey (CERI, 2012) indicated that "these relationships will remain strong .... Career centers must realize that many organizations need their services as talent agents, not event planners" (CERI, 2012, p. 40). Employer relations staff will have to accommodate employer expectations while continuing to support best practices in designing and delivering campus recruitment services and programs. In the next section, we highlight some issues associated with engaging new technology in the employer relations area.

One final recruiting trend has to do with how employer relations staff can reach out to employers who may not visit campus for traditional recruiting events (Carr, 2013) and students with nontraditional employment goals and values (Armstrong, 2013). Reardon, Lenz, Peterson, and Sampson (2012), in their undergraduate career-planning text, described a variety of alternative ways of working. The traditional 8–5 job, remaining with one employer for extended periods of time, and collecting a gold watch are seen as relics of times gone by, never to return. Kamenetz (2012) suggested that the "four-year career" was becoming the new reality for many individuals. Pink (www.danpink.com; 2001), more than 12 years ago, labeled workers in the new economy as being part of the free agent nation, while Feller and Whichard (2005) described these individuals as "knowledge nomads." How do we help someone who wants to work for a web start-up, a digital media studio, or become a social entrepreneur? These types of employment opportunities are not likely to be represented by the traditional employers who attend career fairs and conduct face-to-face interviews. These employers may find candidates through their blogs, web videos, social media, or other personal branding tools. This trend increases the pressure on career services to track trends, especially those related to virtual recruiting and social media (the topic of our next section) and to seek knowledge sources beyond their professional boundaries. Following futurist sites (e.g., www.wfs.org) and blogs, and reading publications such as *Fast Company* and *Kiplinger* can help career services staff be strategic about their approach to connecting today's students with tomorrow's employers.

Virtual Recruiting/Social Media

No discussion of future issues and trends in employer relations would be complete without mentioning social media in all its various forms. There has been an explosion in applications that makes it hard for both employers and career services staff to keep up with the trends and tools (e.g., Hentz, 2007; Kubu, 2012; Shea & Wesley, 2006). ComputerWeekly.com posted an article in 2009 entitled: "Will LinkedIn and Second Life kill the recruitment industry?" (www.computerweekly.com/news/1280096950/Will-LinkedIn-and-Second-Life-kill-the-recruitment-industry). A recent NACE article spoke to this trend by noting that "interacting on social media websites has become a must for colleges and employers" (Giordani, 2012b).

This area has several different facets. One has to do with how employers use social media and virtual tools to reach out to applicants and vice versa (Anders, 2012; Colao, 2012; Lamoureux, 2012). Brotherton (2012) reported social media networks (e.g., LinkedIn, Facebook) have overtaken job boards as the way to recruit candidates for the majority of recruiters. Referrals by current employees were the other highly recommended method. In addition to allowing employers to recruit globally, social media sites allow "employees to alert their personal networks about possible job openings in their organizations" (p. 24). Lamoureux (2012), in his discussion of social media in the hiring process, noted that the issues associated with this type of recruiting have outpaced the ability of the legal process to provide guidance. Watching the outcomes of legal cases in this area, such as whether employers can request access to student's social media sites, will be an ongoing issue for career centers and recruiters to track.

Another issue involving social media has to do with how career centers brand themselves and connect to students using social media (Osborn & LoFrisco, 2012). Career center offices are highlighting their use of social media sites as a way of connecting to their various constituents. Pomona College describes what students can expect from each of the career development office's social media sites: www.pomona.edu/administration/career-development/about-us/social-media.aspx. Employers, career services staff, students, and alumni can use social media to "chat" about job opportunities, recruiting and employment trends, and related topics in a 24/7 environment.

Career center staff must also be knowledgeable in this area to effectively assist students who are seeking employment and internship opportunities. The increase in publications dedicated to this topic (e.g., *Your Social Media Job Search,* Hellmann, 2011; *Job Searching with Social Media for Dummies,* Waldman, 2011), and web posts devoted to this topic, (e.g., "Using Pinterest as a job-search and branding tool", NACE, 2012d) is likely exceeding staff's ability to digest all the information available. Workshops and classes that support student job seeking must effectively incorporate this information so that students make use of all the tools available that will contribute to a successful job search. The University of Kentucky career services office hosted a "social media week," which included a workshop on developing a social media resume and partnered with an employer sponsor to provide free pizza at the event. Any view of career services delivery relating to employment seeking must consider social media and virtual tools as essential components to maintain a competitive advantage.

Summary

As career services go forward into the future, there will be a variety of trends and issues to follow. Many of these are directly tied to the programs and services associated with the employer relations function. Employer relations, in its critical boundary spanning role, is a key component in determining the success of a career services unit. Career centers will always be held accountable for the numbers and types of employers who seek an institution's graduates. Employer relations personnel must constantly develop and nurture these external relationships to ensure a pipeline of opportunities for students seeking both internships and permanent employment.

In addition to cultivating employment opportunities, employer relations staff, along with center directors, are facing the reality that fundraising is a permanent part of their job description. In most cases, career services offices cannot maintain their levels of quality without seeking funds from outside groups, such as employers, as well as other persons (parents, alumni) who place value on the career center's work. Employers continue to represent the most significant external supporter of career services operation and the management of these relations are often key to the kind and level of support for recruitment activities.

As noted above the employer relations unit must consider how the diverse student population may impact its efforts. Groups such as alumni, distance learners, international students, and student veterans require special consideration with regard to how to provide employment preparation services and in enabling them to make connections with prospective employers.

Finally, employer relations programs of the future must adjust to the realities of providing programs and services in a virtual age. These programs must understand how employers engage with social media and virtual technology to find candidates. This technology enables employers to use "just-in-time recruiting" for filling their recruitment needs, rather than planning far in advance for campus visits or attendance at career fairs. Some employers will undoubtedly still use traditional face-to-face methods when it suits their needs, but employer relations personnel will have to adapt to these demands in order to provide effective services for a key stakeholder.

In our collective years, we have weathered many ups and downs in the economy, as well as various institutional challenges (e.g., reduced budgets, turf wars regarding who has the institutional mission for employer relations, increases in student demands for assistance). We have read and seen many scenarios that predicted the end of on-campus recruiting, the demise of face-to-face career expos, and the elimination of position titles/job listings in favor of skill-based recruitment. While certainly factors such as economic downturns, the global workplace, and technology have reshaped the landscape of employer relations, using all the available tools to build effective relationships and link job candidates and employers will continue to be the measure of success for the foreseeable future.

References

Allen, I. E., & Seaman, J. (2012, June). *Conflicted: Faculty and online education, 2012.* Wellesley, MA: Inside Higher Ed, Babson Survey Research Group.

Anders, G. (2012, July 27). How LinkedIn has turned your résumé into a cash machine. *Forbes.* Retrieved from http://www.forbes.com/sites/georgeanders/2012/06/27/how-linkedin-strategy/

Andersen, P., & Vandehey, M. (2012). *Career counseling and development in a global economy* (2nd ed.). Belmont, CA: Brooks/Cole.

Armstrong, B. T. (2013, January 10). Attracting millennial talent: What colleges know … and employers should find out. *Forbes*. Retrieved from www.forbes.com/sites/barbaraarmstrong/2013/01/10/attracting-millennial-talent-what-colleges-know-and-employers-should-find-out/

Bash, R., & Reardon, R. (1986). Fundraising in career development services. *Journal of Career Development, 12*, 231–239.

Behrens, D. (2009). Interview practice U.S. style: A workshop for international students. *Journal of Employment Counseling, 46*, 182–184.

Bolles, R. N. (2013). *What color is your parachute?* New York: Ten Speed Press.

Brotherton, P. (2012). Social media and referrals are best sources for talent. *T+D, 66*, 24.

Bullock, E. E., Braud, J., Andrews, L., & Phillips, J. (2009). Career concerns of unemployed U.S. war veterans: Suggestions from a cognitive information processing approach. *Journal of Employment Counseling, 46*, 171–181.

Carr, A. (2013, March). The world's 50 most innovative companies 2013. *Fast Company*, p. 86–155.

Colao, J. J. (2012, November 14). The Facebook job board is here: Recruiting will never look the same. *Forbes*. Retrieved from http://www.forbes.com/sites/jjcolao/2012/11/14/the-facebook-job-board-is-here-recruiting-will-never-look-the-same/

Collegiate Employment Research Institute (CERI), Michigan State University. (2012). *Recruiting trends 2012–2013* (42nd ed.). East Lansing, MI: Author

Collins, M. (2011, September). The future of the field: 2015. *NACE Journal*. Retrieved from http://www.naceweb.org/j092011/future_trends_2015/

Dine, M., & Bapat, V. (2007). Think and act globally: Career services, international students, and global employers. *NACE Journal, 67*, 21–25.

Dey, F., & Real, M. (2010, September). Emerging trends in university career services: Adaptations of Casella's career centers paradigm. *NACE Journal, 71*, 31–35.

Feller, R., & Whichard, J. (2005). *Knowledge nomads and the nervously employed: Workplace change and courageous career choices.* Austin, TX: PRO-ED, Inc.

Friedman, T. L., (2013, May 28). How to get a job. *New York Times*. Retrieved from www.nytimes.com/2013/05/29/opinion/friedman-how-ro-get-a-job.html?_r=0.

Garis, J. W. (in press). The value proposition. In T. Steinfeld & M. Cantomanolis (Eds.). *Leadership in career services: Voices from the field.* Charleston, SC: Author.

Garis, J., & Dalton, J. (Eds.). (2007). E-portfolios: Emerging opportunities for student affairs. *New Directions for Student Services, 119*. San Francisco: Jossey-Bass.

Giordani, P. (2012a, November). Counseling and hiring student veterans. *NACE Journal, 72*, 34–37.

Giordani, P. (2012b, February). Tracking social media effectiveness. *ACE Journalonline*. Retrieved from www.naceweb.org/j022012/social-media-marketing/?referal=knowledgecenter&menuid=107

Hellmann, R. (2011). *Your social media job search.* New York: Author.

Hentz, M. C. (2007). Using new media: Blogs and social networking technology. *NACE Journal, 67*, 31–33.

Herr, E. L., Heitzmann, D. E., & Rayman, J. R. (2006). *The professional counselor as administrator: Perspectives on leadership and management in counseling services.* Mahwah, NJ: Lawrence Erlbaum Associates.

Herr, E. L., Rayman, J. R., & Garis, J. W. (1993). *Handbook for the college and university career center.* Westport, CT: Greenwood Press.

Institute of International Education. (2012). *Open doors 2012.* New York, NY: Author. Retrieved from www.opendoors.iienetwork.org/

Kamenetz, A. (2012, January 12). The four-year career. *Fast Company*. Retrieved from http://www.fastcompany.com/1802731/four-year-career

Kleinman, A. (2012, November 11). 10 companies that are working to hire veterans. *The Huffington Post*. Retrieved from http://www.huffingtonpost.com/2012/11/11/companies-hiring-veterans_n_2103868.html

Koc, E. (2010, February). Recruiting for tomorrow: Recent trends in employer internship programs. *NACE Journal, 70*, 18–24.

Kubu, E. (2012, April). Career center social media implementation and best practices: Findings of a nationwide survey. *NACE Journal, 72*, 32–39.

Lamoureux, B. J. (2012, September). How social media is changing the hiring game. *NACE Journal, 73*, 8–11.

Miller, G. A. (2012, March 28). Tech talk: Tools for distance engagement. *Spotlight for Career Services Professionals.* Retrieved from http://naceweb.org/s03282012/mobile-social-media-student-engagement/?referal=knowledgecenter&menuid=12

National Association of Colleges and Employers. (2005, Fall). Into the future: Top issues and trends for career services and college recruiting. *NACE Journal, 66*, 27-32.

National Association of Colleges and Employers. (2006). *A student's guide to interviewing with third-party recruiters.* Retrieved from www.naceweb.org/legal/third-party_recruiters/

National Association of Colleges and Employers (2010, May). *2010 Internship & co-op survey research brief*. Bethlehem, PA: Author.

National Association of Colleges and Employers (2011a, April). *2011 Internship & co-op survey research brief*. Bethlehem, PA: Author.

National Association of Colleges and Employers. (2011b, October 26). Job outlook: The candidate skills/qualities employers want. *Spotlight for Career Services Professionals*. Retrieved from www.naceweb.org/s10262011/candidate_skills_employer_qualities/

National Association of Colleges and Employers. (2012a, August 15). Class of 2013: Women, Hispanics driving diversity growth. *Spotlight for Career Services Professionals*. Retrieved from http://naceweb.org/s08152012/diversity-recruiting-women-hispanic/

National Association of Colleges and Employers. (2012b, January). *Principles for third-party recruiters*. Bethlehem, PA: Author. Retrieved from http://naceweb.org/principles/?referal=knowledgecenter&menuID=203#thirdparty

National Association of Colleges and Employers. (2012c, June). *User's guide to the principles for professional practice: Principles for career services professionals*. Bethlehem, PA: Author. Retrieved from www.naceweb.org/principles/guide/

National Association of Colleges and Employers. (2012d, April 25). Using Pinterest as a job-search and branding tool. *Spotlight for Career Services Professionals*. Retrieved from www.naceweb.org/s04252012/pinterest-social-media/

National Center for Education Statistics. (2011). *Military service members and veterans: A profile of those enrolled in undergraduate and graduate education in 2007–2008*. Washington, DC: Author.

Niles, S. G., & Harris-Bowlsbey, J. (2009). *Career development interventions in the 21st century* (3rd ed.). Upper Saddle River, NJ: Pearson.

Osborn, D., Dikel, M. R., Sampson, J. P., Jr., & Harris-Bowlsbey, J. (2011). *The internet: A tool for career planning* (3rd ed.). Broken Arrow, OK: National Career Development Association.

Osborn, D., & LoFrisco, B. M. (2012). How do career centers use social networking sites? *The Career Development Quarterly, 60*, 263–272.

Pink, D. (2001). *Free agent nation: The future of working for yourself*. New York, NY: Warner Books.

Rayman, J. (1993). *The changing role of career services*. San Francisco, CA: Jossey-Bass.

Reardon, R., Lenz, J., Peterson, G. W., & Sampson, J. P., Jr. (2012). *Career development and planning: A comprehensive approach* (4th ed.). Dubuque, IA: Kendall Hunt.

Reardon, R. C., & Lumsden, J. A. (2003). Career interventions: Facilitating strategic academic and career planning. In G. L. Kramer & E. D. Peterson (Eds.), *Student academic services in higher education: A comprehensive handbook for the 21st century* (pp. 167–186). San Francisco, CA: Jossey-Bass.

Salmon, S. S. (2007, May). Legal Q & A. *NACE Journal, 67*, 6–9.

Sampson, J. P., Jr. (2012, October). *Ethical issues associated with information and communication technology in guidance*. Paper presented at the International Association for Educational and Vocational Guidance Conference, Mannheim, Germany.

Shea, K., & Wesley, J. (2006). How social networking sites affect students, career services, and employers. *NACE Journal, 66*, 26–32.

Smith, J. (2012, December 3). Is the career fair dead? *Forbes*. Retrieved from www.forbes.com/sites/jacquelynsmith/2012/12/03/is-the-career-fair-dead/

Stein-McCormick, C., Osborn, D. S., Hayden, S., & Van Hoose, D. (2013). *Career development for transitioning veterans*. Broken Arrow, OK: National Career Development Association.

Venable, M. A. (2011, August). Career services and online colleges: Providing critical support to online students. Retrieved from www.onlinecollege.org/whitepapers/2011-08.pdf

Waldman, J. (2011). *Job searching with social media for dummies*. Hoboken, NJ: John Wiley & Sons, Inc.

Zunker, V. G. (2011). *Career counseling: A holistic approach* (8th ed.). Belmont, CA: Brooks/Cole.

APPENDICES

Appendix A

Sample Staff Titles/Roles within Employer Relations and Recruitment Services

Assistant Director for Development & Outreach

Assistant Director, Employer and Campus Relations

Assistant Director, Employer Connections and Job Preparation

Assistant Director, Employer Connections for Special Populations

Assistant Director for Employer Outreach

Associate Director, Career Connections for Students

Associate Director, Employer Relations & Customer Service

Associate Director, Employer Relations/Development

Associate Director for Employer Services

Counseling Manager, Employer Services

Director of Employer Testing Services

Employer and Alumni Outreach Manager

Employer Relations and Events Coordinator

Employer Relations Manager

Employer Relations Manager, International & Experiential Opportunities

Employer Services Manager

Employment Services and Events Coordinator

Event Marketing & Special Project Coordinator

Job Development Specialist—Employer Relations & Customer Service

Manager of Employer Development

Manager of Employer Relations

Manager, Recruiting Services

Marketing/Employer Relations Assistant

Placement Files and Event Coordinator

Recruiting Coordinator, Employer Relations

Recruiting Facilitator

Recruiting Programs Assistant

Recruiting Programs Coordinator

Recruitment Specialist

Senior Associate Director, Campus Relations & Development

Appendix B
Sample New Employee Orientation Checklist

New Staff Member Orientation: Pre-Arrival Checklist

Director
- Generate offer letter
- Send letter to new staff member
- Send contract to Vice President for signatures
- Notify supervisor that contract has been approved, signed, and returned
- Provide office assistant with copies of signed contract for new staff folder

Office Administrator
- "Prepare Job Offer" via Human Resource system
- Make copy of Personnel Action Form (PAF) for file, supervisor, and employee
- Oversee compilation of new staff packet
- Update staff database

Office Manager
- Order business cards
- Order shirt(s) and nametag
- Prepare sample ID request form (Packet)
- Prepare staff member mailbox

Promotions & Publications Coordinator
- Revise organizational chart
- Print new master staff list

Supervisor
- Generate e-mail to all CC staff, introducing new staff member, including contact info
- Set time for new staff member to meet with Office Administrator to complete back-up paperwork, review timesheet procedures, and review the institution's new employee packet

Systems Coordinator
- Order computer if needed
- Set up personal computer and create access to campus networks
- Order campus e-mail account and configure e-mail
- Update website list/credits
- Update office distribution lists
- Add to in/out "board" system

Appendix B (continued)

New Staff Member Orientation: On-Site Checklist

Supervisor
- Arrange intranet sign-up sheet for new employee to set up meetings with selected staff
- Set initial meeting to discuss:
  - Compiling & submitting data for career center (CC) annual report
  - Unit Policies & CC Office Manual
  - Absence/emergency contact procedures
  - CC historical information
  - Professional association memberships
- Provide office welcome token (e.g., plant, flowers)
- Provide a tour of CC and nearby departments
- Review phone/mail procedures
- Discuss general questions/concerns

Office Administrator
- Review institution's new hire procedures online via "New Employee Checklist" (including orientation procedures)
- Provide and review CC new staff packet
- Review timesheet procedures

Promotions and Publications Coordinator
- Arrange photo for staff board

Associate Director for Administration
- Set up room reservation system account and provide training
- Review key building policies; provide link to electronic copy of building manual

Career Center New Staff Packet
- Copy of contract & Personnel Action Form
- Copier code instructions
- Staff-to-meet sheet
- *Career Center Office Manual*

Appendix C
Sample Employee Evaluation Form

Review of Performance
Administrative and Professional Personnel

Employee's Name [ ] **Title** [ ]

Employee ID [ ] **Department** [ ]

Rating Period [ ] **Through** [ ]

1. Planning
  Perception of opportunities
  Definition of objectives
  Anticipation of problems
  Allocation of resources
  [Excellent ▼]

2. Programming
  Formulation of approaches to meet objectives
  Evaluation and selection of alternatives
  Scheduling target dates for completion
  Sequencing of planned steps
  [Excellent ▼]

3. Organizing
  Recruiting and development of competent staff
  Assignment of responsibility and authority
  Determination of effective structure
  Establishment of effective working relationships
  [Excellent ▼]

4. Leadership
  Initiation of action
  Communication of ideas
  Motivation of others
  Drive and perseverance
  [Above Satisfactory ▼]

5. Operating
  Establishment of procedures and methods
  Performance of planned actions
  Making of satisfactory decisions
  Monitoring and control of operations
  [Excellent ▼]

6. Effectiveness
  Ability to obtain desired results
  Adherence to established schedule
  Performance at planned quality level
  Economy and adherence to budget
  [Excellent ▼]

7. Personal Characteristics
  Can do attitude
  Integrity
  Dependability
  Responsiveness
  [Excellent ▼]

8. Potential
  Promotability
  Capability of learning new skills
  [Excellent ▼]
  - Excellent
  - Above Satisfactory
  - Satisfactory
  - Needs Improvement/Unsatisfactory

Overall Rating [Excellent]

Comments on Rating
[ ]

Employee's Signature _____   Reviewer's Signature _____

Date _____   Date _____

Appendix D
Sample Topics for an Employer Relations Policy and Procedures Manual*

Administrative
Deactivating student/alumni accounts
Recording & disseminating follow-up/destination data
Accessing on-campus interview statistics
Billing and refund procedures (student fees—if any; employer fees); may also include dealing with delinquent accounts
Institutional procedures for handling funds from employers, sponsors
Facebook page policy
Hiring and training procedures for student staff (graduate assistants, student assistants)
Career fair policies (this topic may be an entire section on its own)

Employer Related
Handling job vacancy announcements; posting guidelines, dealing with fraudulent listings
On-campus interviewing schedules
Pre-selection for campus interviews
Hosting employer events (e.g., information sessions, receptions, networking nights), including policies on alcohol at employer events
Employer requests for student data (e.g., lists of graduating seniors in selected disciplines, résumés)
Maintaining employer records (e.g., database procedures, business cards)
Employer cancellations (expos, interview schedules)
Employment offer guidelines
Employer testing
Third party recruitment, soliciting of services, multilevel marketing employers
Hosting employers—parking, welcome signs, etc.
Employer donations/sponsorships

Student Service Related
Credential files; may vary depending on whether files are paper only, both electronic and paper, or exclusively electronic
Eligibility for services (students and alumni)
Student registration procedures/approving accounts/disabling accounts
Dealing with student no shows
Handling student complaints
Managing student protests at career center venues
Sending e-mails to students—events, employer visits, job announcements; important to understand institutional policy on mass e-mails to students
Students with special needs (e.g., on-campus interviewing for students with disabilities)

*Note: Some policies may be covered in a career center–wide office manual; others may be strictly associated with employer relations and recruitment services.

Appendix E
Sample Employer On-Campus Recruiting Evaluation Forms

THE FLORIDA STATE UNIVERSITY | The Career Center *linking futures*

ON-CAMPUS RECRUITING EVALUATION

Please take a moment to complete this brief form. Your feedback is essential to better serve you. Thank you, in advance, for your cooperation.

On-campus Interviewing Evaluation

4-Strongly Agree   3-Agree   2-Disagree   1-Strongly Disagree   N/A-Does Not Apply

Employer Relations and Recruitment Services

1. The following facilities were satisfactory or above my expectations:
    a. Interview rooms — 4 3 2 1 N/A
    b. Employer Lounge — 4 3 2 1 N/A
2. Career Center staff were available throughout the day(s). — 4 3 2 1 N/A
3. Career Center policies regarding on-campus interviewing are clear. — 4 3 2 1 N/A
4. The cleanliness of facilities met my expectations. — 4 3 2 1 N/A
5. Are you the individual who coordinates recruitment activities with FSU? — Yes   No
6. If yes, please answer the following:
    a. Directions to the Dunlap Student Success center were clear. — Yes   No
    b. Parking procedures were clear. — Yes   No
    c. Scheduling procedures were clear. — Yes   No
    d. Scheduling arrangements met my expectations. — Yes   No

FSU Students

1. Students exhibited professionalism in their appearance. — 4 3 2 1 N/A
2. The resumes were professional and presented quality information. — 4 3 2 1 N/A
3. Students presented themselves well and were well prepared for their interview. — 4 3 2 1 N/A
4. Students were knowledgeable of the job description. — 4 3 2 1 N/A
5. Students were knowledgeable of your organization. — 4 3 2 1 N/A
6. FSU students are stronger candidates than students at other institutions where you recruit. — 4 3 2 1 N/A

General Career Center Evaluation

1. How can Career Center staff better serve your on-campus recruiting needs?

2. What other improvements are you able to suggest for the FSU Career Center?

3. What was the most challenging aspect in coordinating your recruiting visit to FSU?

Appendix E *continued*
Sample Employer On-Campus Recruiting Evaluation Forms

Student No Shows
Please list any "no shows" below:

Student Name	Scheduled Date/Time
_____	_____
_____	_____
_____	_____
_____	_____

Academic Preparation of FSU Students
The following comments will be shared with deans/department heads unless you specify otherwise.

1. What attributes (skills, experience, academic preparation, etc.) impressed you most about the candidates?

2. Which academic course offerings prove most beneficial in preparing FSU students for your market?

3. What additional course offerings would better prepare the students for your market?

4. What skills did students lack the most compared to other campuses where you recruit?

Need Additional Information on Other Services?
Your request will be forwarded to the appropriate staff member.

___ Seminole Futures and other Career Expositions
___ Placement Partners/Donor Opportunities
___ Employer Panels and/or Workshops
___ Mock Interview Program
___ Career Portfolio Contest Sponsorship
___ Professional Network (Database of Friends & Alumni willing to provide Career Information

___ Co-op/Internships, Externships, and/or Summer Work
___ MBA/Graduate Student Recruitment Opportunities
___ Florida Career Professional Association Membership
___ Event Sponsorship
___ Dunlap Success Center Room Sponsorship

Your name_____   Your organization_____

Thank you for recruiting at the Florida State University Career Center!

Appendix E *continued*
Sample Employer On-Campus Recruiting Evaluation Forms

Smith Career Center
Recruiter Evaluation Form - SPRING 2013

To help us evaluate our campus recruiting service, please complete this form at the end of the recruiting day and return it to the front desk before leaving. Rate the items using the following scale:

Excellent - 4   Above Average - 3   Average - 2   Below Average - 1   Not Applicable - n/a

Thank you!

CAMPUS INTERVIEW ASSISTANCE

Pre-visit instructions and information............ 4 3 2 1 n/a	Staff assistance for special requests............ 4 3 2 1 n/a
Greeting and assistance on day of visit.......... 4 3 2 1 n/a	Student sign-up process............................. 4 3 2 1 n/a
Luncheon arrangements............................... 4 3 2 1 n/a	Interview facilities..................................... 4 3 2 1 n/a

OVERALL 4 3 2 1

Comments:

STUDENT PERFORMANCE

	BU Students	Students At Other Universities
Student Preparation		
Well-defined, realistic career goals................	4 3 2 1	4 3 2 1
Knowledge of organization and its opportunities........	4 3 2 1	4 3 2 1
Pertinent questions asked............................	4 3 2 1	4 3 2 1
Quality of candidate data sheet or resume............	4 3 2 1	4 3 2 1
Academic preparation.................................	4 3 2 1	4 3 2 1
Communication Skills		
Articulation/grammar/vocabulary.....................	4 3 2 1	4 3 2 1
Poise/handshake/ eye contact........................	4 3 2 1	4 3 2 1
Personal Qualities		
Maturity...	4 3 2 1	4 3 2 1
Decisiveness...	4 3 2 1	4 3 2 1
Knowledge of strengths and weaknesses...............	4 3 2 1	4 3 2 1
Assertiveness		
Leadership Qualities.................................	4 3 2 1	4 3 2 1
Expression of interest and initiative...............	4 3 2 1	4 3 2 1
Confidence...	4 3 2 1	4 3 2 1
Enthusiasm...	4 3 2 1	4 3 2 1
Adaptability		
Willingness to relocate..............................	4 3 2 1	4 3 2 1
Willingness to travel................................	4 3 2 1	4 3 2 1

Comments:

Recruiter Name (Optional) _____   Company _____

Candidates Interviewed: ___ Co-op/Interns or ___ Graduating Students

Bradley University   Peoria, IL 61625   Phone 309/677-2510   Fax 309/677-2611

Appendices

Appendix F
Sample Student Marketing Materials

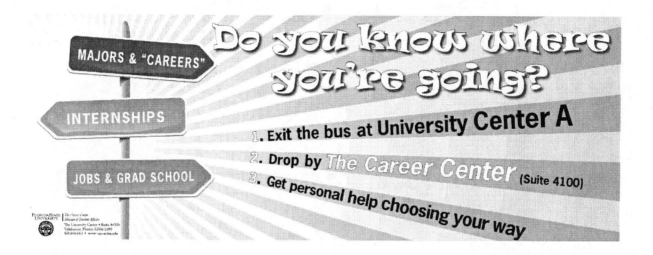

Spring 2012 Events

Part-Time Job Fair
January 12 • 10 a.m. - 2 p.m.
Oglesby Student Union

Engineering Day
(Not Just for Engineering Majors)
January 24 • 9 a.m. - 3 p.m.
FAMU-FSU College of Engineering

Seminole Futures
(All Majors Career Exposition)
January 26
9 a.m. - 12 p.m. and 1 - 3 p.m.
Leon County Civic Center

Health Professions Exposition
February 16 • 11 a.m. - 3 p.m.
College of Nursing Lobby

College of Communication & Information Career Day
March 19 • 1 - 4 p.m.
Alumni Center

Education & Library Career Expo
April 24 • 10 a.m. - 2 p.m.
Oglesby Union Ballrooms

Take the first step by obtaining *Plus!* services through your SeminoleLink account in Blackboard.

For more information on these events and other services, drop by The Career Center, located in the Dunlap Success Center, or visit career.fsu.edu

THE FLORIDA STATE UNIVERSITY

The **Career Center**
linking futures
850.644.6431 • career.fsu.edu

Appendix F *continued*
Sample Student Marketing Materials

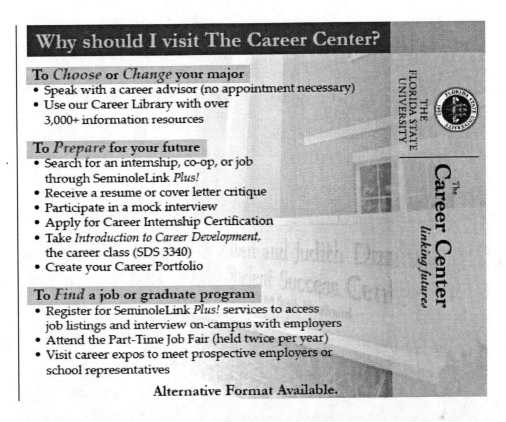

Why should I visit The Career Center?

To *Choose* or *Change* your major
- Speak with a career advisor (no appointment necessary)
- Use our Career Library with over 3,000+ information resources

To *Prepare* for your future
- Search for an internship, co-op, or job through SeminoleLink *Plus!*
- Receive a resume or cover letter critique
- Participate in a mock interview
- Apply for Career Internship Certification
- Take *Introduction to Career Development*, the career class (SDS 3340)
- Create your Career Portfolio

To *Find* a job or graduate program
- Register for SeminoleLink *Plus!* services to access job listings and interview on-campus with employers
- Attend the Part-Time Job Fair (held twice per year)
- Visit career expos to meet prospective employers or school representatives

Alternative Format Available.

THE FLORIDA STATE UNIVERSITY

The Career Center
linking futures

Drop by today, visit our site, or find us on Facebook!

The Career Center is located in the Dunlap Success Center at the corner of Traditions Way and Woodward Avenue.

We're open:
Monday - Friday:
8 a.m. - 5 p.m.

Career advisors are available:
Monday - Friday:
9 a.m. - 4:30 p.m.

Fall & Spring Semesters:
Tuesday hours until 8 p.m.

For more information, visit career.fsu.edu, call 850.644.6431, or search FSU Career Center on Facebook!

Appendix F *continued*
Sample Student Marketing Materials

If you know students searching for jobs or employers looking for new hires, send them to the Career Center!

We work to link employers and students who may be a good fit. The Career Center offers:

- SeminoleLink, an online career management database where employers can post internships, part-, and full-time jobs and students can search for listings that meet their needs.
- Career expositions, held each semester for students to meet and network with employers.
- Resume books and Seminole Profiles, which allow employers to view and request resumes of FSU students and offer students more exposure to employers.
- Professional Network, a database of FSU alumni and friends who have volunteered to provide career, industry, and employment information to students.

For more information, contact Sean Collins at 850.644.2529 or scollins@fsu.edu.

Appendix F *continued*
Sample Student Marketing Materials

2 weeks...

Post-graduation plans still up in the air?
Discuss your options with Career Center staff!

**Leach Center
Wednesday, April 22
1:30 - 3:30 p.m.**

**Recruit diverse, high-quality students
from all disciplines at Florida State University's**

SEMINOLE FUTURES
A CAREER EXPOSITION

Thursday, September 24, 2009 • 9 a.m.-noon & 1-3 p.m.
Tallahassee-Leon County Civic Center
Register at **career.fsu.edu/expos/futures**
by September 3 to avoid a late fee

* Registration fee for corporate employers, $600
Non-profit and government agencies, $400

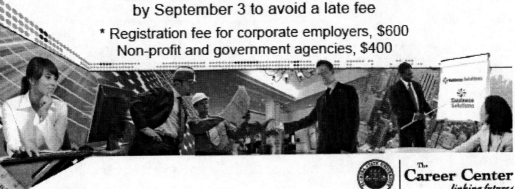

Appendix G
Sample Student/Alumni Career Fair Evaluation Form

Student/Alumni Evaluation
SEMINOLE FUTURES CAREER EXPOSITION Fall 2012

Student/Alumni Evaluation
Seminole Futures Career Exposition

Please circle YES or NO

1. Were you able to meet with employers of your choice?	YES NO
2. Was the event beneficial to you in your job search?	YES NO
3. Would you recommend attending Seminole Futures to others?	YES NO
4. Was Seminole Futures well organized?	YES NO
5. Was your career field adequately represented at Seminole Futures?	YES NO
6. Have you created an "On-line Career Portfolio?"	YES NO
7. If yes…Did creating an online career portfolio help you sell your skills to an employer?	YES NO
8. Was information you received prior to Seminole Futures consistent?	YES NO

How did you learn about Seminole Futures? (Please check all that apply.)

___ Email   ___ FSView

___ Career Center Staff   ___ Student Organization

___ Career Center Materials (flyer, poster, etc.)   ___ Blackboard

___ Career Center Website   ___ Announcement In Class

___ FSU Homepage   ___ Other (Please specify) _____

Are there any comments or suggestions you have for improving Seminole Futures?

Are there any specific employers that you would have liked to have seen represented at Seminole Futures?

PLEASE LEAVE THIS FORM IN THE EVALUATION BOX NEXT TO THE ESCALATORS AT THE
EXIT BEFORE YOU LEAVE TODAY
THANK YOU!!!

Appendix H
Sample Employer Handbook Topics

Employer Services
On-Campus Recruiting
Other Sponsorship Opportunities
Networking Database
Career Center Facebook Page
Resume Books
Resume Referral Service
Job Listing Service
Career Expositions
Additional Career Center Services
On-Campus Recruiting Procedures
Using Our System to Recruit
Department of Accounting Best Practices
Recruitment Calendar

Connect to Campus
Recruit on Campus
Tips for Successful On-Campus Recruiting
Tips for a Successful Career Expo
Key Contacts
Career Center Liaisons
University Contacts
Student Organizations
Partnering with the University

What We Offer
Career Center Room Sponsorship
Sponsorship Programs
Chart of Sponsorship Opportunities

Directions & Lodging
Find the Career Center
Find Expo Locations
Area Hotels & Dining

Your School of Choice
Profile of Students
University Highlights
Graduating Senior Survey
Degrees Awarded for Selected Programs
Salary and Hiring Data
Top 20 Employers by Interviews
Top Employers by Hires
Offers via On-Campus Interview Program
Offer Summary
Offers by Industry Type
Offers by Major
Industry Reference of Employers

Appendix I
Sample Career Fair Employer Evaluation

FLORIDA STATE UNIVERSITY | The CAREER CENTER

Employer Evaluation
Seminole Futures Career Exposition Fall 2012

To assess and enhance the effectiveness of Seminole Futures Career Exposition, we would like to consider your input and comments. Please take a few minutes to complete this evaluation. A Career Center staff member will come by your booth this afternoon to pick up the evaluation or you may fax it to 850-644-3273 by September 28, 2012. Thank you!

Please check the appropriate space:

	EXCELLENT	VERY GOOD	FAIR	POOR
Physical Set-Up	___	___	___	___
Staff/ Volunteer Assistance	___	___	___	___
Registration Form	___	___	___	___
Confirmation Information	___	___	___	___
Student Participation	___	___	___	___
Overall Organization	___	___	___	___
Overall Quality	___	___	___	___

Approximate number of students visiting my table _____

My organization will consider attending the next **Seminole Futures Career Exposition:**   YES   NO

How did your organization learn about Seminole Futures? Please circle one or more of the following options:

Career Center Email	Career Center Flyer	Previous Attendee	Co-worker
Career Center Staff	Career Center Website	Alumni Association	
Facebook.com	Linkedin.com	Other_____	

We would be particularly interested in the:

_____ Spring Leadership & Diversity Event   _____ Professional Network Volunteer Program
                                                        (Provide career information to students and alumni)

_____ Career Planning Class Employer Panel   _____ Mock Interview Programs

_____ Sponsorship Opportunities   _____ Employer Panels/forums

Contact Person _____ Email _____

Name of Organization _____

Appendix J
Sample Employer "Hold the Date" E-Mail

fall 2010 events at the florida state university

Mark your calendars today to participate!
The Florida State University Career Center • Tallahassee, Florida

Career Expositions

Engineering Day • September 15 • FAMU-FSU College of Engineering
Reserve your spot now. Contact Megan Waldeck with questions at 850.644.8625 or mwaldeck@fsu.edu.

Seminole Futures • September 16 • FSU Turnbull Conference Center
Reserve your spot now. Contact Nancy Friedman with questions at 850.644.9772 or nfriedman@fsu.edu.

Day-After Interviews

September 16 and 17 • Dunlap Success Center
Our interview facilities are available to our employers who attend career expositions for day-after interviews.

On-Campus Recruiting

September 27-November 12 • Dunlap Success Center
Reserve your date now. Contact Julia Kronholz with questions at 850.644.6493 or jkronholz@fsu.edu.

Resume Referral Program

Ongoing
We are happy to forward student resumes to you electronically.
Click here for more details. Contact Debbie Crowder with questions at 850.644.4023 or dcrowder@fsu.edu.

Job Listings

Ongoing
If you have an immediate need to fill part-time or full-time jobs, we are happy to post your position.
Click here for more details. Contact Debbie Crowder with questions at 850.644.4023 or dcrowder@fsu.edu.

Employer Relations and Recruitment Services Staff

Myrna Hoover • Program Director, 850.644.6089
Lindsey Katherine • Senior Assistant Director, 850.644.9772
Nancy Friedman • Assistant Director, 850.644.9773
Julia Kronholz • Assistant Director, 850.644.6493

Megan Waldeck • Assistant Director, 850.644.8625
Debbie Crowder • Program Assistant, 850.644.4023
Sean Collins • Credentials Coordinator, 850.644.3459

Quicklinks
FSU Highlights
Employer Handbook
Placement Partners
Career Center Facebook Page

THE FLORIDA STATE UNIVERSITY | The Career Center *linking futures*

Appendix K
Sample Selected Employer Relations Publications

Publication Title	Last Revised	Updated	Owner
Alumni brochure		As needed	
Career Center brochure		As needed	
Career Internship Certification Program handout		As needed	
Internship, Co-op, and Job Shadow bookmark		As needed	
Job Club handout		Fall/Spring	
Mock Interview handout(s)		Fall and Spring	
ProfessionalNole bookmark		As needed	
SeminoleLink/Career Portfolio bookmark		Fall and Spring	
Career Exposition handouts		As needed	
Big Career Guide		Summer	
Career Portfolio User's Guide		As needed	
Conducting Information Interviews		As needed	
Dressing to Impress		As needed	
Finding a Summer Job		As needed	
Finding and Using Graduate Student Resources		As needed	
Interviewing for a Faculty Position		As needed	
Making the Most of Your Internship or Co-op Work Experience		As needed	
Negotiating Job Offers		As needed	
Preparing a Portfolio		As needed	
Preparing for a Telephone Interview		As needed	
Preparing for Internships and Co-ops		As needed	
Preparing for the First Interview		As needed	
Preparing for Your Second Interview		As needed	
Researching Potential Employers		As needed	
Searching for a Job as an International Student		As needed	
Searching for a Job in Human Services		As needed	
Searching for a Job in Tallahassee		As needed	
Searching for a Part-time, Temporary or Seasonal Job in Tallahassee		As needed	
Searching for a Temporary Job		As needed	
Seminole Link User's Guide		As needed	
Starting Your Small Business: An Entrepreneur's Guide		As needed	
Using Proper Etiquette		As needed	
Using the Internet in Your Job Search		As needed	
Working Abroad		As needed	
Writing a Curriculum Vitae		As needed	
Writing Effective Letters		As needed	
Writing a Résumé		As needed	
Employer Handbook		Fall	

Appendix L
Sample Yearly Employer Relations Publications and Events Timeline

AUGUST
Part-Time Job Fair
Employer Promotion:
- Press release

Student Promotion:
- Plasma slide
- Posters
- Yard signs
- Website
- DSA calendar
- Blackboard

Day of Materials:
- Expo guide (map of tables & employer list)
- Table tents for employers
- Signage
- Table tents for dining facilities

Mock Interviewing Material Update:
- Update posters
- Update handouts
- Update mentor training covers

SEPTEMBER
Engineering Day
Promotion:
- Plasma slide
- Posters
- Yard signs
- Website
- DSA calendar
- Blackboard
- Banner

Day of Materials:
- Expo guide (map of tables & employer list)
- Directional signage
- Check in signs
- Table tents for employers

Seminole Futures
Promotion:
- Plasma slide
- Posters
- Yard signs
- Website
- DSA calendar
- Blackboard
- Banner

Day of Materials:
- Expo guide (map of tables & employer list)
- Expo guide large print
- Café sign and table tents
- Job Search Strategies Workshop sign

OCTOBER
Graduate & Professional School Fair Promotion:
- Plasma slide
- Posters
- Yard signs
- Website
- DSA calendar
- Blackboard
- Banner

Day of Materials:
- Table tents for participants
- Expo guide (map of tables & employer list)

JANUARY
Part-Time Job Fair
Promotion – Employers:
- Press release

Promotion – Students:
- Plasma slide
- Posters
- Yard signs
- Website
- DSA calendar
- Blackboard

Day of Materials:
- Expo guide (map of tables & employer list)
- Table tents for employers
- Signage
- Table tents for dining facilities

Mock Interviewing Material Update:
- Update posters
- Update handouts
- Update mentor training covers

Seminole Success Night
Promotion:
- Handouts

Day of Materials:
- Program
- Table tents for employers
- Directional signage

Engineering Day
Promotion:
- Plasma slide
- Posters
- Yard signs
- Website
- DSA calendar
- Blackboard
- Banner

Day of Materials:
- Expo guide (map of tables & employer list)
- Directional signage
- Check-in signs
- Placement Partner welcome signs
- Table tents for employers

Seminole Futures
Promotion:
- Plasma slide
- Posters
- Yard signs
- Website
- DSA calendar
- Blackboard
- Banner

Day of Materials:
- Expo guide (map of tables & employer list)
- Expo guide large print
- Café sign and table tents
- Job Search Strategies Workshop sign

FEBRUARY
Health Professions Fair
Promotion:
- Plasma slide
- Posters
- Yard signs
- Website
- DSA calendar
- Blackboard
- Banner

Day of Materials:
- Expo guide (map of tables & employer list)
- Table tents for employers
- Directional signage

APRIL–JULY
Education & Library
Promotion:
- Plasma slide
- Posters
- Yard signs
- Website
- DSA calendar
- Blackboard
- Banner

Day of Materials:
- Table tents for participants
- Expo guide (map of tables & employer list)
- Signage

JUNE–AUGUST
Career Guide

Employer Handbook

Career Connection

Bookmarks

Career Portfolio Contest:
- Update handouts
- Small guides
- Career Center and Alumni brochures

Workshops
Promotion:
- Plasma slide
- Yard signs
- Directional signage
- Posters
- Website
- DSA calendar

Etiquette Dinner:
- Invitational emails

Appendix M
Sample Employer Sponsorship Opportunities

The Career Center — Sponsorship Opportunities
linking futures

	Single Expo Registration $700	Annual Garnet Placement Partner $3,000	Annual Gold Placement Partner $5,000	Annual Diversity & Veterans Networking Event Sponsorship $7,000 (Each)	Perpetuity Room Sponsor $15,000
Career Expo Registration fees waived (per year)	1	3	4	4	8 (over 2 years)
Extra Expo Participants (Up to 4 per expo)		✓	✓	✓	2 years
Priority Placement at Expo		✓	✓	✓	2 years
Membership on Career Center Advisory Board		✓	✓	✓	2 years
Access to On-line Resume Books		✓	✓	✓	✓
Corporate Name & Logo (with hyperlink to employer website) on Homepage of Career Center Website		✓	✓	✓	✓
Special Recognition on Student Expo Guide & Career Guide		✓	✓	✓	✓
Preferred participation in speaker forums, workshops, classes & mock interviews		✓	✓	✓	2 years
Organization spotlight in student newsletter and on Facebook		✓	✓	✓	✓
Full Page Ad in Career Guide ($2,400 value)		25% Discount	Free	Free	2 years FREE
Use of Dunlap Success Center for information sessions, receptions, etc.			2 events per year	3 events per year	4 events per year
Extra Table at Expo ($250 value)			✓	✓	2 years
Registration Fee waived for Veterans Networking Event and Seminole Success Night			✓	✓	✓
Naming Opportunity				✓	✓
Corporate Logo on Plasmas In Lobby of Recruiting Area & Outside of Interview Suite					✓

Appendix N
Sample Career Center Comment Card

Comments On The Career Center

Please Circle Your Ratings And Share Comments
Using The Following Rating Scale
1/ Strongly Agree 2/ Agree 3/ Disagree 4/ Strongly Disagree

1. I was satisfied with:

    a. Hours of operation 1/2/3/4
       Comments_____

    b. Friendliness of staff 1/2/3/4
       Comments_____

    c. Quality of staff assistance 1/2/3/4
       Comments_____

    d. Quality of information/resources 1/2/3/4
       Comments_____

    e. Facilities 1/2/3/4
       Comments_____

    f. Quality of assistance 1/2/3/4
       Comments_____

    g. Overall contacts 1/2/3/4
       Comments_____

2. Was this your first visit? _____Yes _____No
3. The Career Center could be improved by _____
   _____
   _____

4. Date of Visit ___/___/___ Time of Visit_____
5. Service Location
      University Center_____
      College of Business_____
      College of Engineering_____

Thank You For Your Comments

Appendix O
Sample Student Veterans Career Services Information Sheet

FSU Student Veterans

Link to Your Future...

Take advantage of The FSU Career Center services:

- Speak with a career advisor to clarify your career goals and employment or educational targets
- Get help connecting your prior experience and skills to future opportunities
- Learn strategies for researching employers and conducting an effective job search
- Develop a resume and professional e-portfolio to highlight your skills and achievements
- Use our SeminoleLink database, containing over 30,000 employers, that can help you explore internships, part-time, and full-time employment
- Network with alumni and friends of FSU through ProfessioNole
- Attend career expos and other networking events
- Participate in the Mock Interview Program

Contact Information

FSU Veterans Center

 Veterans.fsu.edu

 Main: 850-645-0028
Becky Culp: 850-645-9867

Collegiate Veterans Association

 Veterans.fsu.edu/Collegiate-Veterans-Association

 E-mail: CVAFSU@gmail.com

 Find us on Facebook: Collegiate Veterans Association

 Twitter: @CVAFSU

For more info, visit our site at: **career.fsu.edu**

INDEX

A
Academy of Management, 15
accountability, 73-74
    return on investment (ROI), 73, 77
advisory boards, 59, 62, 71
Aldridge, M., 2
Allen, I., 77
alternative ways of working, 79
alumni associations, 51, 55, 76
alumni networks, 10, 13, 33, 51-52, 76
American College Personnel Association
    (ACPA), 3, 5
Anders, G., 80
Andersen, P., 76
Andrews, L., 78
annual reports, 64-66
Arminio, J., 55
Armstrong, B., 79
Association of Graduate Careers Advisory
    Services, 3
Association of School and College Placement, 4

B
Bank of America Career Services at the
    Pennsylvania State University, 60
Bapat, V., 77
Bash, R., 54, 74
Behrens, D., 77
benchmarking, 62, 66, 68
Bertoch, S., 8
Bolles, R., 79
Bowling Green University, 79
Bradley University's Smith Career Center, 66
Braud, J., 78
Brotherton, P., 80
Bullock, E., 78

C
Canadian Institute for Career Center
    Management, 38
career center mission, 7
career fairs, 25
    boutique, 8, 25-26
    budgeting, 27
    employer evaluation, 98
    employer fees, 57
    establishing target audience, participants, 27
    event evaluation, 30
    event follow-up, 31
    event management, 11, 13
    event registration, 30-31
    final event preparation, 29
    locating a venue, 27
    marketing checklist, 28
    marketing to employers, 27
    marketing to students, 28
    multiple schools, 26
    partnering with campus groups, 26
    student/alumni evaluation form, 96
    tips for a successful event, 30
    training event staff, 29
    recruiting and using volunteers, 29
career services council, 9
CareerShift, 50
Carnegie Mellon career partner program, 59
Carr, A., 79
Carvalho, S., 38
Casey, M., 68
Center for Credentialing and Education Centers
    of Career Development Excellence, 68
Cheney, M., 3
Chervenik, E., 2, 5
Civil Rights Act of 1964, 2
Clinton, L., 55
Colao, J., 80
Collegiate Employment Research Institute
    (CERI), 11, 12, 57, 75, 77, 78, 79
College Central Network (CCN), 20, 46, 50
College Placement Annual, 4
College Placement Council, 4
Collins, M., 76
comment card, 66
    sample, 103
Council for the Advancement of Standards in
    Higher Education (CAS), 15, 46, 62, 68
    CAS Standards for Technology and System
    Implementation, 47
CPC Salary Survey, 4
Credential Agent, 31

Index

credentials service, 31
   private vendors, 31
   waiver of right to access, 32
CSO Research Inc., 20, 46, 49, 50
   Solutions for Career Services, Co-op & Internship Offices, 20
Curran, S., 7

D

Dalton, J., 74
Davidson, M., 51
de Oliveira, M., 38
Dey, F., 2, 8, 78
Dikel, M., 77
Dine, M., 77
DirectEmployers Association, 20, 50
distance learners, 77
diversity and leadership programs, 34-35
Domkowski, D., 67
Donald, G., 38
Duke University's School of Business, 8

E

Eastern College Personnel Office, 3
Edds, C., 28, 38, 40, 43, 44
employee evaluation form sample, 87
employer branding, 40
employer fees, 53
employer handbook sample topics, 97
employer-in-residence programs, 33
   activities for, 33-34
employer relations, 1-2
   adoption of technology systems, 3
   current mission and philosophy, 5
   development of professional organizations & publications, 3
   emphasis on networking, 2
   fundraising, 54
   history, 1-2
   organizational structure, 7-8
      centralized vs. decentralized career services, 7-9, 63-64, 74, 75
   policy & procedures manual sample topics, 88

program management, 7, 9
   events management, 11-12
   policies and procedures, 16
   staffing, 10-11
promotion of career development, 5
publications list, 100
publications and events timeline, 101
relationship management, 40-41
sample job description, 13
sample staff job titles, 84
shift in mission, 2
job-hunting groups, 2
employer sponsorship opportunities sample sheet, 102
events management, 11, 17
Experience, 20, 46, 49, 50

F

Facebook, 28, 38, 40, 46, 80, 88
Fast Company, 80
Feller, R., 79
Florida State University, 75, 76
   Alumni services, 76
   Career Center, 15, 50, 51, 56, 62, 64, 66, 67, 68, 71
      Office Manual, 15
      organization chart, 11
   Internships, International Programs office, 75
Folsom, B., 71
Friedman, T., 74
fundraising, 8, 54, 74
   alternative funding sources, 54-55
   career services naming, 60
   employer-based fund generation, 55, 56
      employer displays, 58
      employer partner programs, 58
      facility room sponsors, 60, 61
   employer fees, 56
      advertising, 56
      career fairs, 57
      job or internship postings, 58
      program or event sponsorship, 58
      space utilization, 58
      specialized services, 56
   institutional support for, 56

Index

locus of funding in career services
    continuum, 54
    partnerships, 55, 59
    student fees, 54-55
    unsolicited donations, 60
future issues and trends, 73

G

Garis, J., 1, 7, 8, 54, 74
Geisler, B., 1, 2
George Mason University
    Career Services, 65
    School of Management, 8
George Washington University, 40
Giordani, P., 1, 2, 3, 4, 38, 46, 78, 80
Going Global, 49, 50
graduate students/peer assistants, 13
Green, M., 13
Gysbers, N., 2

H

Harpster, G., 55
Harris-Bowlsbey, J., 76, 77
Harvey, E., 67
Harwick, G., 4
Hayden, S., 78
Hegi Family Career Development Center at Southern Methodist University, 60
Heitzmann, 7, 36, 45, 54, 62, 73
Hellmann, R., 80
Hentz, M., 80
Herr, E. 1, 7, 8, 10, 13, 16, 36, 45, 46, 50, 51, 53, 54, 55, 60, 62, 63, 73, 74, 75
Herrick, R., 4
How to Market Career Development Programs and Services, 43, 44

I

information systems, 45
informational interviewing, 33
Institute of International Education, 77
Interfolio, 31, 50
international students, 77-78
internships, 12, 63, 74-75
    funding for internships, 75
InterviewStream, 50
Iowa State University, 8, 9

J

Jackson, E., 67
Job Choices, 4
job development, 12, 16, 25
job postings, 24
    charging for, 24
    fraudulent postings, 24
    granting access to job postings, 25
    history of job postings, 45
    increasing the number of job postings, 25
    systems for job posting, 46, 58
Job Searching with Social Media for Dummies, 80
Jones, C., 55
Journal of Career Planning and Employment, 4
Journal of College Placement, 4
just-in-time recruiting, 81

K

Kamenetz, A., 74, 79
Kansas State University, 79
Kirts, E., 1
Kleinman, A., 78
Kiplinger, 80
Knoll, J., 2
knowledge nomads, 79
Koc, E., 75
Kubu, E., 36, 80
Kuk, L., 54
Krueger, R., 68

L

Lamoureux, B., 80
Lavruski, V., 33
Lenz, J., 10, 13, 16, 45, 67, 71, 76, 79
liaisons, 14, 21, 41-42, 76
LinkedIn, 33, 39, 40, 46, 76, 80
Linnenburger, J., 71
Loffredo, S., 14
LoFrisco, B., 80
Louisiana State University Career Services, 66
Loveys, K., 1
Lucas, E., 2
Lumsden, J., 74

Index

M

Makela, J., 62, 66, 70, 71
Marketing, 36
    cost-effective marketing strategies, 42-43
    employer branding, 21, 24, 40
    key questions to ask, 40, 43
    return on investment, 39
    sample employer "hold-the-date" e-mail, 99
    sample marketing coordinator job description, 36-37
    sample student marketing materials, 92-95
    staff, 12, 13, 14, 26, 29, 36, 37, 38, 84,
    targeting relevant employers, 39
    to administrators, faculty, and staff, 41-42
    to employers, 27, 39
    to students, 28, 36
MBA Career Services Council, 15
Miami University in Ohio's Career Services, 63
Michelin Career Center at Clemson, 60
Michigan State University, 67
Middle Atlantic Placement Association, 3
Midwest College Placement Association, 3
Miller, G., 77
mission statements, 5, 62, 63-64
Mitchell, F., 4
MonsterTrak, 50
Multi-School Environment, 51, 52

N

National Association for Legal Professionals (NALP), 15
National Association of Appointment Secretaries, 3
National Association of Colleges and Employers (NACE), 4-5, 14, 62
    Career Services Benchmark Survey, 8, 11, 36, 38, 46, 68
    Career Services Professional Outcomes Committee, 68
    Evaluation Standards, 9
    Evaluation Workbook, 9-10, 15
    Guidelines for Internal and External Review of Career Services, 69, 70
    Internship & Co-op Survey, 75
    Job Outlook 2011 Survey, 19
    NACE Journal, 4
    NACELink Network, 20, 50
    Principles for Professional Practice, 3, 20
    Principles for Third-Party Recruiters, 79
    Professional Standards, 54, 69
    Recruiting Benchmarks Survey, 19
    regional associations, 4-5
    Student's Guide to Interviewing with Third-Party Recruiters, 79
National Association of Graduate Career Advisory Services, 3
National Association of Placement and Personnel Officers, 3
National Association of Student Personnel Administrators (NASPA), 14
National Association of Workforce Development Professionals (NAWDP), 14
National Career Development Association (NCDA), 5, 10, 14, 62
    Career Counseling Competencies, 10, 70
National Center for Education Statistics, 78
National Employment Counseling Association (NECA), 14
Nell, A., 14
new staff member orientation checklist, 85-86
New York University Career Center, 75
Niles, S., 76
Nord, D., 2

O

on-campus recruiting, 12, 19-20
    bidding, 22
    communicating with students and employers, 23
    employer evaluation, 89, 90, 91
    focus of, 19
    handling cancellations, 22
    hosting employers on campus, 23-24
    information sessions and receptions, 23
    interview selection procedures, 21
    international students, 77
    management of, 12
    open sign-up, 22
    preparing for employer visits, 23
    preselection, 21
    scheduling interviews, 20

Index

Ohio State University, 8
Oregon State University, 59
Osborn, D., 77, 78, 80

P
Panke, J., 13
Parsons, F., 45
partnership programs, 52
Penn State Career Services, 63, 65, 71
Peterson, G., 10, 16, 45, 76, 79
Phillips, J., 78
Pierson, D., 1
Pink, D., 79
Pinterest, 46, 76, 80
placement offices, 1-2
policies and procedures, 16
    developing employer policies, 39, 88
    employer polices on career services website, 17, 79
    fundraising policies, 56
    systems policies, 47, 52
Pomona College, 80
Portland State University, 78
Powell, C., 1
Princeton Review, 68
Principles for Professional Practice, 3
ProfessioNole, 51-52, 76
program assessment and evaluation, 62
    advisory boards, 71
    annual reports, 64, 66
    benchmarking, 68
    comment forms, 66
    employer hires, 65
    executive summaries, 66
    external reviews, 69
    focus groups, 68
    graduating senior surveys, 67
        guidelines, 67
    learning outcomes, 66, 70
    minimal to maximal approaches to program evaluation, 62
    needs-based surveys, 66-67
    outcome-based, 70-71
    satisfaction data, 66
    self-audits, 68

professional networking databases, 33, 51-52
professional organizations, 3- 5, 14
professional publications, 3-5

R
Rayman, J., 1, 7, 8, 36, 45, 54, 62, 67, 70, 71, 73, 74
Real, M., 2, 78
Reardon, R., 7, 8, 10, 16, 45, 54, 67, 71, 74, 76, 79
recruiting evaluation forms, 89-91
recruiting trends, 78-80
recruitment program activities, 19
regional placement and recruitment organizations, 3
Rentz, A., 2
resume referrals, 25
Rocky Mountain College Placement Association, 3
Rook, D., 68
Rooney, G., 62, 66, 70, 71
Rotary clubs, 39

S
Salmon, S., 78
sample organizational chart, 11
Sampson, J., 10, 14, 16, 45, 52, 65, 76, 77, 79
School and College Placement, 4
Schutt, D., 7, 16
Seaman, J., 77
Second Life, 80
Shamdasani, P., 68
Shea, K., 80
skills needed by employers, 19
Smith Career Center at Bradley University, 60, 66
Smith, J., 79
Smith, K., 8
social media, 13, 40, 80-81
Society for Human Resource Management (SHRM), 15, 39
Southern Methodist University, 59
Southern College Placement Association, 3

Index

special populations, 75-78
    alumni, 76-77
    distance learners, 77
    diverse student groups, 76
    international students, 77-78
    veterans, 78
staffing, 10-11
    benchmarking staff competencies, 15
    new employee orientation, 14
    promoting staff professional growth, 15
    staff evaluation, 15
    staff training and development, 14
Stein-McCormick, C., 78
Stewart, D., 68
St. Lawrence University, 78
student success stories, 38
Sweet Briar College Career Services, 66
Sweeten, E., 4
Symplicity, 20, 46, 50
    Career Service Manager (CSM), 20

T

talent development, 12, 41, 57, 75, 79
Teal, E., 4
technology, 45
    alternative revenue streams to support technology, 53
    current premier systems, 46
    factors to consider in selecting a system, 46-48
    funding sources, 52-53
    history of in employer relations, 45-46
    partnering with technology, 51
    return on investment, 51
    technologies employed at career centers, 51
Texas A & M University, 55
Texas Exes, 76
Texas State University, 41
Texas Woman's University, 77
third party recruiters, 79
Title VII, 2
Toastmasters, 39
Toppel Career Center at University of Miami, 60
Tull, A., 54
Twitter, 38, 46

U

UCLA Career Center, 63
University of California-Berkeley, 67
University of Cincinnati, 66
University Counseling and Placement Association, 3
University of Florida, 40, 66
University of Illinois at Urbana-Champaign, 8
University of Iowa, 66
University of Kentucky, 80
University of Maryland, 60
University of Michigan, 60
University of Missouri, 67
University of Montana, 77
University of North Carolina-Chapel Hill, 55
University of Texas at Austin, 8
University of Wisconsin-Green Bay Career Services, 67
U.S. Department of Labor, 78

V

Vandehey, M., 76
Van Hoose, D., 78
Venable, M., 46, 77
Vernick, S., 7, 8, 54
veterans, 1, 2, 13, 78
    career services information sheet, 104
Vinson, B., 8
virtual recruiting, 80
Vocations Bureau, 45
Vokac, R., 3, 5

W

Waldman, J., 80
Wasserman Center for Career Development, 60
Web 2.0, 45
Wendover, R., 54
Wesley, J., 80
Western College Placement Association, 3
Whichard, J., 79

Y

Your Social Media Job Search, 80

Z

Zunker, V., 76

Index

Index